JOHN WESLEY

CASCADE COMPANIONS

The Christian theological tradition provides an embarrassment of riches: from Scripture to modern scholarship, we are blessed with a vast and complex theological inheritance. And yet this feast of traditional riches is too frequently inaccessible to the general reader.

The Cascade Companions series addresses the challenge by publishing books that combine academic rigor with broad appeal and readability. They aim to introduce nonspecialist readers to that vital storehouse of authors, documents, themes, histories, arguments, and movements that comprise this heritage with brief yet compelling volumes.

TITLES IN THIS SERIES:

Reading Augustine by Jason Byassee
Conflict, Community, and Honor by John H. Elliott
An Introduction to the Desert Fathers by Jason Byassee
Reading Paul by Michael J. Gorman
Theology and Culture by D. Stephen Long
Creation and Evolution by Tatha Wiley
Theological Interpretation of Scripture by Stephen Fowl
Reading Bonhoeffer by Geffrey B. Kelly
Justpeace Ethics by Jarem Sawatsky
Feminism and Christianity by Caryn D. Griswold
Angels, Worms, and Bogeys by Michelle A. Clifton-Soderstrom
Christianity and Politics by C. C. Pecknold
A Way to Scholasticism by Peter S. Dillard
Theological Theodicy by Daniel Castelo
The Letter to the Hebrews in Social-Scientific Perspective
    by David A. deSilva
Basil of Caesarea by Andrew Radde-Galwitz
A Guide to St. Symeon the New Theologian by Hannah Hunt
Reading John by Christopher W. Skinner
Forgiveness by Anthony Bash
Jacob Arminius by Rustin Brian
Reading Jeremiah by Jack Lundbom
John Calvin by Donald McKim

JOHN WESLEY

Optimist of Grace

HENRY H. KNIGHT III

 CASCADE *Books* • Eugene, Oregon

JOHN WESLEY
Optimist of Grace

Cascade Companions 32

Copyright © 2018 Henry H. Knight III. All rights reserved. Except for brief quotations in critical publications or reviews, no part of this book may be reproduced in any manner without prior written permission from the publisher. Write: Permissions, Wipf and Stock Publishers, 199 W. 8th Ave., Suite 3, Eugene, OR 97401.

Cascade Books
An Imprint of Wipf and Stock Publishers
199 W. 8th Ave., Suite 3
Eugene, OR 97401

www.wipfandstock.com

PAPERBACK ISBN: 978-1-62564-838-9
HARDCOVER ISBN: 978-1-4982-8690-9
EBOOK ISBN: 978-1-5326-4639-3

Cataloguing-in-Publication data:

Names: Knight, Henry H., 1948–, author.

Title: John Wesley : optimist of grace / by Henry H. Knight III.

Description: Eugene, OR : Cascade Books, 2018 | Series: Cascade Companions 32 | Includes bibliographical references.

Identifiers: ISBN 978-1-62564-838-9 (paperback) | ISBN 978-1-4982-8690-9 (hardcover) | ISBN 978-1-5326-4639-3 (ebook)

Subjects: LCSH: Wesley, John, 1703–1791. | Grace (Theology)—History of doctrines. | Holiness—Christianity. | Sanctification—Christianity. | Perfection—Religious aspects—Christianity.

Classification: BT761.3 .K6544 2018 (paperback) | BT761.3 .K6544 (ebook)

Manufactured in the U.S.A.   02/27/18

*To my wife
Eloise,
for her unfailing encouragement
and support*

CONTENTS

Introduction: An Optimism of Grace | ix

1 The Quest for Holiness | 1
2 The Search for Salvation | 9
3 The Moravian Controversy | 23
4 The Calvinist Controversy | 31
5 Proclaiming the Way of Salvation | 41
6 Restoring the Image of God | 59
7 The Means of Grace | 73
8 Relieving the Distress of the Neighbor | 91
9 The Later Controversies | 105
10 Renewing the Face of the Earth | 126
    Conclusion: The Triumph of Love | 141

Bibliography | 147

INTRODUCTION
An Optimism of Grace

JOHN WESLEY IS PERHAPS the most influential theologian of the eighteenth century. This is easier seen from our vantage point than that of his contemporaries. In his own day Wesley was commonly considered a divisive and somewhat marginal figure within the Church of England. Although recognized as a prime mover in the eighteenth century awakening, he was still seen as the leader of an Arminian side branch of what was then a revival largely led by Calvinists.

Today historians consider Wesley and his Calvinist contemporary Jonathan Edwards as the pre-eminent theologians of that awakening, together laying the foundation for a Protestant evangelicalism that would flourish in the next two centuries.[1] Wesley is also the father of Methodism, which now includes 75 million adherents across the globe[2] in over a hundred denominations. In addition, he provided the theological impetus for the Holiness movement that

1. See for example Noll, *Rise of Evangelicalism*.
2. Cracknell and White, *World Methodism*, 1.

emerged in the nineteenth century, both in and outside of Methodism.³ If he is seen, as many do, as also foundational to Pentecostalism, then his contemporary impact is enormous.⁴

Although he sought simply to proclaim the "scripture way of salvation," Wesley developed a distinctive theological vision that formed and shaped a new Protestant tradition. While firmly grounding his theology in scripture, Wesley drew upon a wide array of prior and contemporary sources to assist his interpretation of scripture. Prominent among these were patristic Christianity, Wesley's own Anglican tradition, moderate Puritans, continental Pietism, and the testimonies of others to their experience of God. The result was a theology that emphasized the love of God in Christ, universality of grace, present power of the Holy Spirit, and hope for a new life centered and grounded in love.

To spread this message Wesley employed a connection of lay preachers to travel throughout Great Britain. Those who responded to the message were brought together in small groups called classes, centered on enabling persons to follow a set of spiritual disciplines. If the Wesleyan message drew thousands in England, it found even more fertile soil across the Atlantic. Indeed, in the nineteenth century, Methodism would become the dominant form of Christianity in America.

For his part, Wesley never intended to form a new denomination. He saw the mission of his Methodists as "not to form any new sect, but to reform the nation, particularly the Church, and to spread scriptural holiness over the land."⁵ Yet this understanding of Methodism as a renewal

3. For a fine survey see Dieter, *Holiness Revival*.

4. As argued by Synan, *Holiness-Pentecostal*; Hollenweger, *Pentecostalism*; Martin, *Pentecostalism*; and Knight, *Aldersgate to Azusa*.

5. "Minutes of Several Conversations," Q 3, in *Works* (J) 8:299.

Introduction

movement came under increasing stress in the latter part of the eighteenth century. Wesley's methods were seen as "irregular," perhaps even illegal, by many in the Church of England. Meanwhile Methodism itself began to develop an ethos and identity distinct from the Church of England. Methodism became a separate denomination in America during Wesley's lifetime, in the aftermath of the American Revolution. Methodism in England became separate in the decade after Wesley's death.

Historians have long recognized Wesley as an accomplished evangelist and organizer, but it has not been until the twentieth century that he has been reclaimed as a serious theologian. The groundwork for a reassessment of Wesley's theology began with a series of works by George Croft Cell (1935), William R. Cannon (1946), Harold Lindstrom (1950), Colin Williams (1960), Mildred Bangs Wynkoop (1972), and especially Albert C. Outler (1964, 1975). The year 1975 also marks the publication of the first volume of the Bicentennial Edition of *The Works of John Wesley*, consisting of 35 volumes that contain a wealth of interpretative information for a new generation of scholars. This, along with a renaissance in Wesley studies by both historians and theologians, has already borne fruit in three major contemporary interpretations of Wesley's theology by Randy L. Maddox (1994), Theodore Runyon (1998), and Kenneth J. Collins (2007) plus a host of more specialized books and articles.

Part of the difficulty in seeing Wesley as a serious theologian was due to assumptions about the form and purpose of theology. As Randy Maddox has argued, from the late medieval period on, theology was increasingly understood as an academic discipline pursued "for its own sake" with the goal of attaining "systematic coherence."[6] Among

---

6. Maddox, "Untapped Inheritance," 22.

Introduction

Protestants the ideal model was John Calvin's *Theological Institutes* and the tightly logical systems of the post-Reformation Lutheran and Reformed scholastics. That Wesley never produced a work of this kind was seen as indicating a lack of theological rigor.

But Wesley was an Anglican theologian. Unlike theology on the European continent, Wesley's tradition was influenced by the early church for which theology emerged "in the pastoral context of shepherding the formation of Christians for their lives in the world."[7] Wesley's theological writing, like that of many of his fellow Anglicans, took the form of sermons, essays, letters and prayers, as well as apologetic writings to defend his theology and practice in response to critics. Theology for Wesley did not have the goal of producing a theological textbook but was more like a map pointing to God and showing the way of salvation.

To say his theology did not take the form of a system is not to say it is eclectic or disorganized. At its heart, Wesley's theology is centered on the relationship of love and grace: love as both the governing attribute of God and the content and goal of the Christian life, and grace as the action of God enabling persons to receive and grow in a new life of love.

Recent interpreters have emphasized one or both of these two foci. Randy Maddox argues that consistency in Wesley's theology is due to an "orienting concern" for "responsible grace," that is, a concern to maintain both that without grace we cannot be saved, and because grace is enabling but not coercive, salvation requires our participation.[8] Kenneth Collins sees the conjunction of "holiness and grace" as the "axial theme" of Wesley's theology with

---

7. Ibid., 21.

8. Maddox, *Responsible Grace*, 19.

Introduction

each of the two elements also a conjunction: holiness as holy love, and grace as both free and co-operant.⁹

While these insights are essential to understanding Wesley's theology, they do not in my opinion fully account for his distinctive theological vision. For that we must look more closely at the goal of salvation, as well as grace as the means to attaining that goal.

While in his day (as in ours) salvation was often understood in terms of attaining a happy afterlife, Wesley's focus was firmly on the present: "By salvation I mean . . . a present deliverance from sin, a restoration of the soul to its primitive health, in original purity; a recovery of the divine nature."¹⁰ This recovery of the divine nature Wesley termed "full salvation," while he used "salvation" to encompass the entire process of its recovery.

Wesley's more common terms for full salvation were "Christian perfection" and "entire sanctification." Wesley believed that the promise of salvation was at its heart a promise to restore us to the image of God in which we were created, but had lost when humanity fell into sin, and to be so restored in this life. As God is love, we were meant to have love as our governing disposition, as the fount of our motivation and desire. To be restored to that image would mean we could fully obey the two great commandments given by Jesus Christ, to love God with all our heart, soul, and mind, and to love our neighbor as ourselves.

The teaching of the possibility of Christian perfection in this life was the most distinctive and controversial element of Wesley's theology. It was an especially radical claim for a Protestant. While Catholic and Orthodox theologies could envision something like this for a select

9. Collins, *Theology of John Wesley*, 6.
10. "A Farther Appeal to Men of Reason and Religion," Part I, ¶ I. 3, *Works* 11:106.

group of people—usually those who had left everyday life behind to be solely focused on God—they could do so only because they believed that in spite of the fall into sin there remained in persons a capacity for God upon which grace could do its work of restoration. But Protestants had a more thoroughgoing doctrine of original sin, in which no portion of human nature was untouched by sin. Their focus was on our being declared righteous rather than actually becoming so. Even if one did speak of a measure of growth in the Christian life, for most Protestants something like Christian perfection would necessarily be reserved for the life to come.

How, then, could a Protestant like John Wesley claim that salvation culminates in Christian perfection in *this* life (unlike most Protestants), and also that it is available to *everyone* (unlike most Catholic and Orthodox theologians)? The answer is found in his understanding of grace as the transforming power of the Holy Spirit.

As we have noted, Protestants have understood grace most centrally as an unmerited declaration of forgiveness of sins, grounded solely on the atonement of Jesus Christ. Wesley certainly was in agreement with this. But he added to that an understanding of grace as the work of the Spirit. In "The Witness of Our Own Spirit," a sermon based on 2 Cor 1:12, Wesley said,

> By "the grace of God" is sometimes to be understood that free love, that unmerited mercy, by which I, a sinner, through the merits of Christ am now reconciled to God. But in this place it rather means that power of God the Holy Ghost which "worketh in us both to will and to do of his good pleasure." As soon as ever the grace of God (in the former sense, his pardoning love) is manifested to our soul, the grace of God (in the latter sense, the power of his Spirit) takes place

Introduction

therein. And now we can perform, through God, what to man was impossible."[11]

As we will see, Wesley actually envisioned a transforming work of the Spirit all along the way of salvation. It is also the theological key for how Wesley could move from a Protestant doctrine of original sin to the promise of Christian perfection in this life.

It is this "optimism of grace,"[12] in connection with the goal of perfection in love, that gives Wesley's theology its inner dynamic. That it proved attractive to so many is not only due to its resolute focus on God's love revealed in Jesus Christ, but on the power of the Holy Spirit to enable us to love as God does. This is not only a theology of love and grace, but also at its heart a theology of hope, a promise of new creation in the midst of this present age.

DISCUSSION QUESTIONS

1. What did John Wesley mean by "salvation"?
2. How was Wesley an "optimist of grace"?

---

11. "The Witness of Our Own Spirit," ¶ 15, *Works* 1:309.
12. Rupp, *Principalities and Powers*, 12. This concept is also utilized in Williams, *John Wesley's Theology Today*.

1

THE QUEST FOR HOLINESS

ANGLICAN AND PURITAN ROOTS

THE ROOTS OF JOHN Wesley's spirituality lie in his childhood,[1] where he had the good fortune to be raised in a household in which he was nurtured in a rich heritage of Christian teaching and practices. His parents were Samuel and Susanna Wesley.[2] Samuel was an ordained priest of the Church of England assigned to the rural parish of Epworth. John Wesley shared family life with a large number of siblings. While Susanna gave birth to nineteen children, only ten survived: seven daughters and three sons.

Samuel and Susanna were "High Church" Anglicans who strongly supported the polity, traditions and practices

1. The most thorough recent accounts of John Wesley's life are Collins, *John Wesley*, Heitzenrater, *Wesley and the People Called Methodists*, and Rack, *Reasonable Enthusiast*.

2. Recent biographies of Susanna Wesley are Newton, *Susanna Wesley and the Puritan Tradition*, and Rogal, *Susanna Annesley Wesley*. A recent biography of Samuel Wesley is Torpy, *Prevenient Piety*.

of the Church of England and emphasized frequent participation in Holy Communion. Their devotion to the Church of England would be strongly echoed by their children. But it was in sharp contrast to the views of Samuel and Susanna's own parents.

Both of their fathers—John Westley and Dr. Samuel Annesley—were ordained clergy of a more Puritan persuasion. The origins of Puritanism lie in the brief reign of Queen Mary (1553–58), in which her attempt to restore Roman Catholicism and her persecution of Protestants led many to flee to the European continent for safety. When her Protestant sister Elizabeth ascended to the throne, these Marian exiles returned with a decidedly Calvinist theology and a zeal to purify the Church of England of all vestiges of Roman Catholicism. Consistent with a Calvinist approach to biblical interpretation, they argued the Church should not have any practice for which there was no clear scriptural warrant. Thus they opposed clerical robes, stain glass windows, the giving of rings in marriage, and the celebration of Christmas. Many questioned the legitimacy of an episcopal polity or that the monarch is the head of the Church.

While Puritans demanded that the Church be changed in more Calvinist ways, there were traditionalists who just as ardently wanted to draw the Church back to its Roman Catholic roots. Recognizing this conflict as a threat to the order and stability of the nation, Elizabeth sought to bring an end to the dispute through enforcing a *via media* in which the Church of England would be broadly but decidedly Protestant in doctrine while continuing many of the traditional practices the Puritans opposed. Her *via media* was ably defended by Richard Hooker, whose *Of the Laws of Ecclesiastical Polity* (1595) became foundational for mainstream Anglican theology well into Wesley's day. Hooker argued against the Puritans that the Church is free to have any practice as long as it proves to be beneficial and is not prohibited by scripture. This more moderate and less rigid understanding would be embraced by most in the Church, including John Wesley.

While broad in its scope, this Elizabethan Settlement was not acceptable to those with strongly Puritan or Catholic sympathies. Elizabeth was excommunicated by Pope Pius V, an act that instead of undermining her authority had the effect of solidifying the separation of the Church of England from Rome. Meanwhile, Puritan agitation for change continued unabated.

As the monarchs who followed Elizabeth exhibited leanings toward Roman Catholicism, tension with the Puritans continued to rise. A Puritan army controlled by Parliament overthrew the monarch in 1640 and installed Oliver Cromwell as Lord Protector. But popular discontent with strict Puritan rule plus the seeming disintegration of social order led to the restoration of the monarchy in 1661. Parliament enacted laws restoring the Elizabethan Settlement, and clergy who refused to conform were now removed from their pulpits. These often formed new independent or "Dissenting" congregations. Both of John Wesley's grandparents were ejected from their churches in 1662, and both started new congregations. Dissent would receive legal protection in the Act of Toleration (1689), but its adherents remained second-class citizens, being barred from the universities, holding public office, or voting.

The Puritans not only sought reform of the Church but reform in human lives. They produced a vibrant spirituality centered in the daily reading of scripture and prayer. While Samuel and Susanna embraced High Church Anglicanism over against their parents' nonconformity, they readily followed these Puritan spiritual practices and taught them to their children. When Susanna spent time every week with each of her children, it was this mix of Anglican and Puritan spirituality that shaped how she passed on to them the faith and trained them in spiritual practices.

When they reached the age of ten, Samuel Wesley sent his three sons—Samuel Jr., John, and Charles—to board at Charterhouse School in London, in preparation for attending Oxford University. John began at Oxford in 1720; his younger brother Charles in 1726. Their time at Oxford would be a major turning point in both of their lives.

THE HOLY LIVING TRADITION

For John, that turning point was 1725, when he began reading works in the "holy living" tradition. The first of these was the spiritual classic *The Imitation of Christ* by the medieval monk Thomas à Kempis. Its impact on Wesley was enormous. Writing in the 1760s, Wesley said that upon reading Kempis

> the nature and extent of *inward religion*, the religion of the heart, now appeared to me in a stronger light than it ever had done before....
> I saw that "simplicity of intention, and purity of affection," one design in *all* we speak and do, and one desire ruling all our tempers, are indeed the "wings of the soul," without which she can never ascend to the mount of God.[3]

Also that year Wesley read Bishop Jeremy Taylor's *Rules and Exercises for Holy Living* (1650), which underscored the need for holiness of heart and provided a set of strict rules for attaining it. Among other things this led Wesley to begin keeping a diary.

Wesley completed his masters degree in 1727. Having been ordained a deacon in 1725, he would become an

---

3. "A Plain Account of Christian Perfection," ¶ 3, *Works* 13:137.

ordained priest in the Church of England in 1728. It was a year earlier that he accepted his father's invitation to return to Epworth to serve as curate, and to assist Samuel in the completion of his scholarly commentary on the Book of Job. Although the two years with his father were happy ones for John, they were a financial strain. Before coming to the parish John had been elected a fellow at Lincoln College, Oxford, in which he served as tutor to paying students. When the head of Lincoln College wrote John to call him to return to Oxford to fulfill his obligations, he readily did so.

Upon his return he was asked to provide guidance for his younger brother Charles (1707–88)[4] and one or two of his fellow students who had agreed to meet together regularly for prayer and study. Their faithfulness at worship led others to call this little group the "sacramentarians." One of the students, William Morgan, encouraged the group to join his work in visiting in the prison and ministering to the poor. Although small, the group's activities did not remain unnoticed, and elicited a series of labels from its detractors, most notably the "Holy Club."

In addition to the focus on the poor and imprisoned, two other events would have a lasting impact on Wesley and later Methodism. The first was his reading in 1730 the newly published *Serious Call to a Devout and Holy Life* by Wesley's older contemporary William Law, and a year or so later, Law's *Christian Perfection*. "These," Wesley later wrote, "convinced me more than ever, of the impossibility of being *half a Christian*; and I determined, through his grace, (the absolute necessity of which I was deeply sensible of) to be *all-devoted* to God, to give him *all* my soul, my body, and my substance."[5] The writings of Law underscored

---

4. Recent biographies of Charles Wesley are Tyson, *Assist Me to Proclaim*, and Best, *Charles Wesley*.

5. "A Plain Account of Christian Perfection," ¶ 4, Works 13:137.

and deepened what he had learned from Kempis and Taylor. However, his reading of Law also encouraged Wesley to come to see assurance of salvation as resting upon the cornerstone of his effort to keep the law of God, a theological misunderstanding that would compromise his quest for holiness until 1738.

RESTORING PRIMITIVE CHRISTIANITY

The second significant event was when John Clayton (1704–73) joined the Holy Club in 1732. Although his association with the group was brief, his impact on Methodism was lasting. Besides introducing Wesley to his circle of booksellers and publishers, Clayton's scholarly interest in primitive Christianity was eagerly adopted by Wesley. Emulating what was then believed to have been the common practice of early Christians, the discipline of the Holy Club took on a new rigor, including regular fast days.

The desire to revive primitive Christianity, understood as especially that of the first three centuries of the church, was a common theme of High Church Anglicans. The Oxford Methodists, as they were now being called, began under Clayton's influence to read William Cave's *Primitive Christianity* as well as works by Anthony Horneck and the French Catholic Claude Fleury. These works, which influenced Wesley's theology and practice throughout his life, emphasized the holiness, unity, charity, and devotional disciplines of the early church.[6] Although Wesley would later question the idyllic portrait of primitive Christianity in these writings, he would continue to see it as a model for Methodism.

---

6. Hammond, *John Wesley in America*, 33–34. For more on the influence of Anthony Horneck on Wesley and Anglicanism in general, see Kisker, *Foundation for Revival*.

The Quest for Holiness

While High Church Anglicans sought to appropriate for their day the piety, unity and sacramentalism of primitive Christianity, they were divided over whether to accept the Glorious Revolution of 1688, when the Roman Catholic leaning James II was removed as King by Parliament, to be replaced by William and Mary. Those strongly committed to a divinely ordained hereditary line of succession refused to sign an oath of allegiance to the new monarch, and these "Non-jurors" were then dismissed from their positions in the government or the Church of England.

This political dispute divided High Church Anglicans, including John Wesley's parents. In 1702 Susanna's refusal to say "Amen" after Samuel read the prayer for the king led to a six-month separation. Whatever her views were immediately after the Glorious Revolution, Susanna's letters during the separation clearly show her Non-juror sympathies. It was less than a year after Samuel and Susanna's reconciliation that John Wesley was born.[7]

The Non-jurors especially produced a great deal of scholarly work on primitive Christianity. John Clayton was not only part of this Non-juror community of scholars, but drew Wesley into its more narrow and extreme "Essentialist" or "Usager" wing led by his friend Thomas Deacon. Essentialists like Deacon sought to reform Church of England liturgy by restoring "usages" from the 1549 Book of Common Prayer that had been dropped from the 1662 revision, such as the mixing of water with wine in the cup and the prayer for the Holy Spirit over the elements. But in addition to this, they desired a more radical revision of the 1549 prayer book itself through adopting liturgies and practices found in the *Apostolic Constitutions*. Although scholars

---

7. For more on this story see Hammond, *John Wesley in America*, 16–17; and Heitzenrater, *Wesley and the People Called Methodists*, 29–30.

today believe it is of fourth century Syrian Christian origin, and in Wesley's day most High Church scholars doubted there was ever one single apostolic liturgy, Essentialists were convinced the *Apostolic Constitutions* was the purest expression of the liturgical teaching of the apostles.[8] Wesley would soon have an opportunity to put this restorationist vision into practice.

What we see at Oxford, then, is many of the enduring features that would mark the later Wesley's theology and practice, but also some misunderstandings that would lead him into theological and spiritual difficulties. The practice of spiritual disciplines in a group to which one is accountable would endure, as well as the sharing of the gospel with others and care for the poor. Wesley would continue to see Methodism as a revival of primitive Christianity, but the form that it would take would change considerably. Above all, Wesley's theology would be governed by the quest for holiness, or Christian perfection, but his linking of assurance of salvation with sincerity of effort would undergo a radical change. Still, it is no wonder that in his *Ecclesiastical History* (1781) John Wesley could aptly term those years at Oxford as "the first rise of Methodism."

DISCUSSION QUESTIONS

1. What impact do you think John Wesley's parents had on his early development?
2. As influenced by the holy living tradition, how did Wesley understand what it meant to be a Christian?
3. What did John and Charles Wesley learn from their involvement in the Holy Club?

---

8. Hammond, *John Wesley in America*, 27, 29.

2

THE SEARCH FOR SALVATION

GEORGIA: AN EXPERIMENT IN PRIMITIVE CHRISTIANITY

WITH THE DEATH OF his father Samuel in 1735 and, perhaps to John Wesley's relief, the pastorate at Epworth being given to another, Wesley gladly continued his work at Oxford. But a new opportunity soon opened: Wesley was invited to become a volunteer missionary to England's newest colony, Georgia (established in 1732). With the support from the Society for the Promotion of Christian Knowledge (SPCK), John and three companions—his brother Charles, Benjamin Ingham, and Charles Delamotte—set sail for Georgia in October, 1735.

As Geordan Hammond succinctly put it, "Georgia became the laboratory where Wesley implemented his vision of primitive Christianity."[1] Even on board the ship, the

1. Hammond, *John Wesley in America*, 41.

four compatriots continued the practices of the Holy Club. Once in Savannah, John Wesley would begin to reshape the worship and devotional life of the colony. While being the parish priest involved the larger portion of Wesley's ministry, he was also to reach out to native Americans with the gospel.

But it is important to note that for Wesley at that time, restoring primitive Christianity and missionary outreach to native Americans were means to a larger end. Wesley's chief motive in going to America, he wrote, "is the hope of saving my own soul."[2] It was through preaching the gospel to native Americans that Wesley believed he would gain a deeper understanding of it himself. His work in Georgia thus would lead to his full conversion—that is, perfection in love—and that in turn would make him all the more useful as a missionary.

Wesley's efforts at reform were varied. In some cases, he sought to strictly enforce the rubrics of the 1662 Book of Common Prayer. But he also restored practices from the 1549 prayer book, and even more radically, from the *Apostolic Constitutions* itself. Such practices were unheard of by the colonists and many proved to be controversial.

One area of significant conflict was baptism. Wesley insisted, contrary to most in the Church of England, on rebaptizing Dissenters (a position he would later abandon). He also opposed the popular practice of private baptisms, insisting they occur in the church. Most controversial of all was his insistence on enforcing the rubric in the 1662 prayer book that infants be baptized by trine immersion which evoked strong opposition from some parents.[3]

---

2. "Letter to John Burton," October 10, 1735, *Works* 25:439.

3. A detailed discussion is found in Hammond, *John Wesley in America*, 112–18.

The Search for Salvation

While Wesley's precisionism regarding rules and apostolic precedent were the chief causes of discontent among some colonists, his introduction of hymns into public worship also created opposition. Wesley had come to love hymn singing from hearing the Germans use it in their worship both on board the ship and in Georgia. In 1737 Wesley, working with a printer in Charleston, South Carolina, published *Collection of Psalms and Hymns*, half of which were written by the Baptist Dissenter Isaac Watts, and the remainder from largely Anglican and German Pietist sources. Wesley used the hymnal not only in society meetings but also in worship, a marked departure from the normal Anglican practice of lining the Psalms, in which a leader would sing out one at a time a line from a Psalm and the congregation would attempt to sing it in response. The introduction of these hymns would be one of the complaints lodged against Wesley by his Georgia opponents, but hymnody would become central to later Methodism and the evangelical awakening.[4]

Another feature of Wesley's ministry in Georgia that had a lasting impact were the societies that met in Savannah and for a short while in Frederica. The group in Frederica, where Charles Wesley was based, was begun by the Wesley brothers in June of 1736, but with Charles' return to London in July the society began to lose impetus and had ceased meeting by the end of the year. It was while John was in Frederica that Benjamin Ingham discovered a society already meeting in Savannah, led by the parish clerk Robert Hows. Wesley and Ingham added mutual instruction and exhortation to the group's practice of reading, praying, and singing Psalms. After Ingham's return to England, in February of 1737, Wesley became even more involved in the

4. Ibid., 103–7.

society, and it continued to thrive until John Wesley himself left for England in late 1737.[5]

It is this society in Savannah that Wesley called the "second rise of Methodism,"[6] containing "the first rudiments of the Methodist societies"[7] yet to come. While similar in many respects, these societies were also different from Oxford Methodism. Besides their use of hymns, Hammond notes that while "the Oxford groups ... involved academic study and promoted ministry to the surrounding community, the Georgia societies were primarily devotional. And unlike Methodist bands and Anglican societies, Wesley included women and men together in the same gatherings."[8] Elements from both Oxford and Georgia would be found in later Methodist societies.

Wesley's societies were controversial as some considered them divisive. Adding further to the discontent was Wesley's ministry to women and advocacy on behalf of the poor. As Hammond observes concerning Wesley,

> That women were spiritually equal to men was taken for granted and there is no indication that the opposition he faced in Georgia had any effect in altering this basic assumption.... His advocacy for the poor and oppressed was conceived of as a manner of acting in imitation of Christ and the primitive church in defense of the marginalized. In an unstable frontier environment, it had the predictable result of causing public conflict.[9]

---

5. Ibid., 139–47; and Heitzenrater, *Wesley and the People Called Methodists*, 69–73.

6. "A Short History of the People Called Methodists," ¶ 9, *Works* 9:430.

7. Ibid., ¶ 6.

8. Hammond, *John Wesley in America*, 148.

9. Ibid., 189.

The Search for Salvation

Yet the single event that moved discontent to active opposition was the Sophia Hopkey incident. Hopkey was the eighteen-year-old niece of the colony's chief magistrate, Thomas Causton. Wesley tutored Hopkey in French, provided spiritual guidance, and fell in love with her. But Wesley, who had resolved to remain single prior to his departure for Georgia, was reluctant to propose marriage, fearing it would compromise his ministry and his unreserved commitment to God. Wesley struggled with what to do, and in the face of his continued indecision, Hopkey notified Wesley of her intention to marry William Williamson. Their marriage three days later in South Carolina was irregular, not only because it was outside their parish but was in violation of the requirement in the Book of Common Prayer that an intended wedding should be announced in the church the three prior consecutive weeks.

Initially distraught, Wesley soon became convinced that Hopkey had been dishonest with him prior to her marriage. At the same time, the new Mrs. Williamson became infrequent in her attendance at morning prayer and the Lord's Supper. In July, 1737, he confronted her with these concerns, all of which she failed to acknowledge. Her failure to confess her faults, along with her failure to inform Wesley of her intention to take communion as required by the prayer book, led to Wesley barring her from the sacrament in August.[10]

Causton was infuriated by Wesley's action, and his ire was not eased when Wesley also supported the claims of colonists who accused Causton of overcharging them for goods from the public store. Causton called a grand jury

10. Detailed accounts, although with different emphases, can be found in Hammond, *John Wesley in America*, 176–77; Collins, *John Wesley*, 70–74; Heitzenrater, *Wesley and the People Called Methodists*, 76–78; and Rack, *Reasonable Enthusiast*, 124–33.

13

to investigate the complaints against Wesley, about half of whose members were Dissenters who disliked Wesley's High Church Anglicanism.[11] Wesley was indicted on ten counts, including his treatment of Sophia Williamson, insisting on the baptismal immersion of infants, and refusal to hold a burial service for an Anabaptist.[12] Probably to Mr. Causton's dismay, the grand jury also looked into the complaints about him, resulting in a list of grievances against his conduct.[13]

Wesley's response to the indictments was to escape to South Carolina from which he could return to London to plead his case directly to the colony's Trustees. While not accepting most of the accusations against Wesley, the Trustees were more than happy to receive his resignation from his missionary commission.

In retrospect much was learned as a result of Wesley's ministry in Georgia. His belief in the importance of societies for Christian growth was reinforced and deepened. He also became aware of the power of hymnody as critical to Christian formation and worship. And as he began to recognize that there was no single model of liturgy and discipline in primitive Christianity, his devotion to the early church could move from a legalistic precisionism to a more fruitful focus on apostolic faith, life and mission. But that is in retrospect. During his return to England, Wesley was in despair. He wrote in January, 1738, while on board ship.

> I went to America to convert the Indians, but Oh! Who shall convert me? Who, what is he that will deliver me from this evil heart of unbelief?

11. Hammond, *John Wesley in America*, 169. Heitzenrater describes the grand jury as "rigged" (*Wesley and the People Called Methodists*, 77).

12. Heitzenrater, *Wesley and the People Called Methodists*, 77–78.

13. Hammond, *John Wesley in America*, 169–70, 186.

> I have a fair, summer religion . . . but let death look me in the face, and my spirit is troubled.[14]

Wesley had not found the assurance he was seeking, nor had he attained the holiness he desired. His announced goal of going to Georgia, to save his own soul, was unmet.

Yet Georgia would also play a role in resolving Wesley's spiritual anguish as well as provide the missing piece to his developing theology. For it was in going to Georgia he first encountered German Pietism.

PIETISM: RECOVERING TRUE CHRISTIANITY

Pietism[15] spoke directly to John Wesley's concerns. Emerging among German Lutherans in the late seventeenth century, Pietism emphasized holiness of heart and life, bringing persons together into small groups, and evangelistic and compassionate outreach to others. Yet its strong rootage in the Protestant Reformation would provide Wesley with a crucially different perspective on faith and assurance.

The most important precursor to Pietism was Johann Arndt (1555–1621) whose *True Christianity* Wesley read in Georgia and later abridged for inclusion in his *Christian Library*. Inspired (like Wesley) by Thomas à Kempis among others, Arndt argued that Christianity was not only about forgiveness through Christ but Christ living within.

Drawing on Ardnt, Philip Jakob Spener (1635–1705) began to propose an alternative to the formal confessionalism of the state churches and the polemical rationalism of the reigning Protestant scholastic theologies. Emphasizing the work of the Holy Spirit within, Spener spoke of

14. "Journal, 1" January 24, 1738, *Works* 18:211.
15. For excellent surveys of Pietism see Olson and Collins-Winn, *Reclaiming Pietism*; Shantz, *Introduction to German Pietism*; Brown, *Understanding Pietism*; and Lindberg, *Pietist Theologians*.

salvation in terms of faith as a gift of God; justification as forgiveness and adoption; and a new birth that recreates us in God's image, enabling our participation in the divine nature. Spener formed small groups for the renewal of the larger church (*ecclesiola in ecclesia*), called for renewed piety in his influential book *Pia Desideria* (*Pious Desire*, 1675), and promoted the new movement through extensive correspondence.

The Pietist movement had several branches, all of which were major influences on Wesley. The main branch was centered at the University of Halle, which Spener had founded, and led by his leading disciple, August Herman Francke (1662–1727). Francke believed that conversion must be deeply felt, narratable, and is necessarily preceded by a penitential struggle (*Busskampf*). Francke is also known for establishing a wide range of social institutions, including a school for orphans, a theological institute, and the first modern Bible society. In this Francke would be later emulated by some of Wesley's Methodists.

Johann Albrecht Bengel (1687–1752) was a leader of Württemberg Pietism and, as a leading New Testament scholar in the eighteenth century, was a pioneer in using modern critical methods. His *Gnoman Novi Testamenti* (*Exegetical Notes on the New Testament, 1742*) was a highly influential scholarly work and a major source for Wesley's own New Testament commentary.

In contrast to the Halle mainstream were the Moravian Brethren and their leader, Count Nicolaus von Zinzendorf (1700–1760).[16] Although Spener was his godfather and he had been a student of Francke's, Zinzendorf grew up hav-

---

16. On Count Zinzendorf see Lewis, *Zinzendorf*; and Freeman, *Ecumenical Theology*. On the Moravian Brethren see Sommer, *Serving Two Masters*; and Podmore, *Moravian Church in England*, as well as the surveys of pietism listed above.

ing a personal relationship with Christ. Hence, he rejected the need for a penitential struggle as the prelude to conversion. In 1721 Zinzendorf purchased an estate in Saxony as a refuge for oppressed and persecuted people throughout Europe. By 1722 lay evangelist Christian David was bringing persecuted followers of John Huss (1372–1415) from Moravia to settle on the estate, which was called Herrnhut (Watched by the Lord). Although the largest group, these Moravians were joined by many others who were fleeing persecution.

The summer of 1727 was a crucial time in the life of this diverse and sometimes contentious group of refugees. In July they covenanted together to become a distinct religious society, organizing into small groups called bands. Then in August, they experienced an intense outpouring of the Holy Spirit while receiving the Lord's Supper, bringing a new sense of unity. Their commitment to world mission was what led a contingent of Moravians to be on board the same ship in 1735 that brought John and Charles Wesley to Georgia.

THE ROAD TO ALDERSGATE

On route to Georgia the ship encountered three major storms, all of which underscored in the starkest manner Wesley's assessment of his spiritual state. He was "much ashamed of my unwillingness to die," he wrote in reaction to the first storm, "O how pure in heart must he be, who would rejoice to appear before God at a moment's warning."[17] Reflecting on the second storm, "I could not but say to myself, 'How is it that thou hast no faith?' being still unwilling to die."[18] In this we can see that Wesley continued

17. "Journal 1," January 17, 1736, *Works* 18;141.
18. Ibid., January 23, 1736, *Works* 18:142.

to link attaining a high degree of purity of heart with having a faith that provides an assurance of salvation.

But it was the third and most violent of the storms that pointed Wesley toward a resolution. The storm had raged for seven hours when Wesley went to the Moravian worship service. Noting their humility and refusal to retaliate when ill-treated, (signs of purity of heart), the storm provided an opportunity to see "whether they were delivered from the spirit of fear, as well as from that of pride, anger, and revenge" (a sign of assurance).

> In the midst of the psalm wherewith their service began, the sea broke over, split the main-sail in pieces, covered the ship, and poured in between the decks, as if the great deep had already swallowed us up. A terrible screaming began among the English. The Germans calmly sung on.[19]

Wesley asked one afterwards if either he or their women and children were afraid, and the answer was no, they were not afraid to die. These Moravians had the assurance that Wesley lacked.

While in Georgia Wesley had opportunity to have extensive conversations with the Moravians and the Salzbergers, a body of Pietists in the tradition of Spener and Francke who had fled Catholic persecution in their homeland. While learning from both (and in the long run having more in common with the mainstream Pietists), at this stage it was the Moravians who would have the greatest impact on Wesley's emerging theology.

Like Wesley, the Moravians saw themselves as recovering and embodying apostolic Christianity, but were doing so in ways quite different from Wesley and his colleagues. This is especially the case with their understanding of faith.

---

19. Ibid., January 25, 173, 1736, *Works* 18:143.

The Search for Salvation

When Wesley invited the Moravian bishop, A. G. Spangenberg, for advice concerning his conduct, Wesley related the conversation as follows:

> He said, "My brother, I must first ask you one or two questions. Have you the witness within yourself? Does the Spirit of God bear witness with your spirit, that you are a child of God?" I was surprised and knew not what to answer. He observed it and asked, "Do you know Jesus Christ?" I paused and said, "I know he is the Saviour of the world" "True," replied he; but do you know he has saved you?" I answered, "I hope he has died to save me." He only added, "Do you know yourself?" I said, "I do." But I fear they were vain words.[20]

Back in London, the question of how one comes to have faith and assurance was foremost on Wesley's mind. There the Wesley brothers made the acquaintance of a Moravian named Peter Böhler. It was Böhler who decisively convinced Wesley that he lacked the faith by which one is saved,[21] and over time described for Wesley "the nature of faith; namely, that is (to use the words of our Church) 'a sure trust and confidence which a man hath in God, that through the merits of Christ his sins are forgiven, and he is reconciled to the favour of God.'"[22] Wesley still struggled with Böhler's claim that this faith comes instantaneously as a gift of God, but a fresh study of the New Testament coupled with the testimonies of persons who had received this

---

20. Ibid., February 7, 1736, *Works* 18:146.
21. "Journal 2," March 4, 1738, *Works* 18:228.
22. Ibid., April 22, 1738, *Works* 18:233–34.

faith persuaded Wesley that this teaching was also correct.[23] Not long after, Böhler convinced Charles Wesley as well.[24]

What John Wesley came to realize was that for many years he was depending on his own righteousness—his attempts to resist sin, to do good, and to be faithful in spiritual practices—rather than in what God had done for our salvation in the cross of Jesus Christ. He had been struggling, careening between momentary joy and despair, rather than having an abiding peace and joy. Even when, upon returning from Georgia, he knew his need for faith, he meant by this "only faith in God, not faith in and through Christ."[25] Now he determined to pray for that faith that enables one to trust in Jesus Christ.

It was Charles Wesley who first came to have this faith. Sick with pleurisy, he heard someone enter his room and say "In the name of Jesus of Nazareth, arise, and believe, and thou shalt be healed of all thy infirmities." A Mrs. Turner had been inspired by a dream to speak these words to him. Charles wrote that after hearing those words he felt "a strange palpitation of heart," and "said yet feared to say, 'I believe, I believe'"[26] He found himself at peace with God and rejoicing in Christ.

This was on May 21, 1738. Three days later, on May 24 occurred the most well-known event in John Wesley's life:

> In the evening I went very unwillingly to a society in Aldersgate-Street, where one was reading Luther's preface to the Epistle to the Romans. About a quarter before nine, while he was describing the change which God works in the heart through faith in Christ, I felt my heart

23. Ibid., April 23, 1738, *Works* 18:234.
24. Ibid., May 3, 1738, *Works* 18:237.
25. Ibid., May 24, 1738, ¶ 11, *Works* 18:247.
26. Charles Wesley, *Manuscript Journal*, 106.

strangely warmed. I felt I did trust in Christ, Christ alone for salvation: And an assurance was given me, that he had taken away *my* sins, even *mine*, and saved *me* from the law of sin and death.[27]

Böhler had taught Wesley that this faith in Christ would produce two fruits: "Dominion over sin, and constant peace from a sense of forgiveness."[28] He had brought others to testify "of their own personal experience, that a true faith in Christ is inseparable from a sense of pardon for all past, and freedom from all present, sins.[29] This now fit with Wesley's own experience: he not only had an assurance of salvation, but while before he had struggled against sin, often unsuccessfully, now he was always able to overcome.[30]

During the decade to follow Wesley would need to sort through conflicting claims by various Moravians concerning whether or not there are degrees of faith or degrees of assurance, as well as the extent of the dominion over sin one receives when one has faith in Jesus Christ. Among other things, this would lead Wesley to make more careful distinctions between the new birth and Christian perfection, and between the faith of a servant prior to justification and the faith of a child of God afterward.

But in a fundamental way Aldersgate resolved for Wesley the relation of assurance to holiness. Assurance was not, as he had thought, a result of attaining holiness of heart but instead accompanied faith given as a free gift of God, based on the cross of Christ and a work of the Holy Spirit in us. That this gift came instantaneously decisively altered Wesley's understanding of how God works, not replacing

27. "Journal 2," May 24, 1738, ¶ 14, *Works* 18:249–50.
28. Ibid., ¶ 11, *Works* 18:247–48.
29. Ibid., ¶ 12, *Works* 18:248.
30. Ibid., ¶ 16, *Works* 18:250.

his former belief in a gradual work, but integrating the instantaneous with it. In short, he developed a much greater sense of the power of God at work in human lives.

Some might have thought that having received an assurance of salvation, Wesley would abandon his quest for holiness of heart and life. Why seek Christian perfection if assurance comes as a free gift? But Wesley remained convinced that true Christianity ultimately consisted in attaining perfection in love, and salvation in restoring persons to the image of God. What the Moravians contributed to Wesley's theology was not an alternative to seeking holiness but the key to how it is attained. Justification and the new birth were the foundation that made growth in sanctification possible.

Before Aldersgate Wesley had sought holiness as a means to personal assurance. Now he was free to grow in love for God and neighbor not to receive anything, but as a grateful response to the gift he had received of God's love for him in Jesus Christ.

DISCUSSION QUESTIONS

1. John Wesley's time in Georgia is often considered a failure. Do you agree? What do you think Wesley learned there that would shape his future ministry?

2. What was the impact of Pietism on Wesley? Would it be accurate to describe Wesley himself as an Anglican Pietist?

3. What happened at the prayer meeting on Aldersgate Street? What difference did it make for Wesley's life and ministry?

3

THE MORAVIAN CONTROVERSY

JOURNEY TO THE CONTINENT

ALTHOUGH ALDERSGATE WAS A theological and spiritual turning point for Wesley, he did not emerge from it untroubled. The source of some of his unease was the teaching of the Moravians in England concerning the nature and extent of assurance and the new heart that accompanies justification by faith. This would be further compounded when the English Moravians advanced a further teaching concerning means of grace such as prayer, scripture and the Lord's Supper.

Wesley summarized these teachings in two points:
1. "That a man *can't have any degree* of justifying faith till he is wholly freed from all doubt and fear, and till he

has (in the full proper sense) a new, clean heart."

2. "That a man *may not use* the ordinances of God, the *Lord's Supper* in particular, before he has such a faith as excludes all doubt and fear, and implies a new, a clean heart."[1]

Wesley would come to emphatically deny both of these assertions, but, with regard to the first, he would not do so without considerable inward struggle. In his own experience following Aldersgate Wesley found his faith was interrupted by doubt, and knew that while sin no longer had the power in his life it once did, he had not attained Christian perfection. That being the case, this first teaching of the Moravians in England would mean Wesley did not have justifying faith at all.

Thus it was this first teaching that was foremost in his mind when he left in June 1738 to visit the Moravians in Germany. There Wesley was able to have extensive conversations with Count Zinzendorf, Christian David, and many others whose testimonies he recorded in his Journal. What he found was that the common teaching in Germany was considerably different from that among the Moravians in England. Count Zinzendorf, for example, noted that justification brought peace "but not always joy"; and argued that assurance is distinct from justification, so that one might not know until later that one is justified.[2] Christian David described the new birth not as the elimination of inward sin but as an end to its controlling power in one's life: "though it did not *reign*, it did *remain* in me; and I was continually *tempted*, though not *overcome*."[3] Wesley would later make

---

1. "Journal 2," Preface, ¶ 10, *Works*.
2. Ibid., July 9, 1738, *Works* 18:261.
3. Ibid., August 10, 1738, *Works* 18:274.

these same distinctions in describing the new birth in his own theology.

While he would continue to think and rethink these theological distinctions in relation to scripture and his own spiritual experience, Wesley's trip to Germany provided him with many of the ideas that would help him by the mid-1740s to develop his mature theology of salvation. But about a year after his return to England Wesley would face a much more serious conflict with a Moravian teaching.

THE FETTER LANE CONTROVERSY

It was in early May of 1738, just a few weeks prior to Wesley's attendance at the Aldesgate prayer meeting, that Peter Böhler and John Wesley formed the Fetter Lane Society in London. It brought together Methodists and Moravians in a common weekly meeting for mutual confession, exhortation, and prayer. With Böhler leaving a few days later, John Wesley would become the primary leader. John Wesley identified the founding of this society as "the third rise of Methodism."[4]

The Fetter Lane Society had flourished while Wesley was in Germany, and continued to do so after his return. But when in the Spring of 1739 the Wesley brothers began to be frequently absent from London to preach in other cities and towns, the society began increasingly to fall under Moravian influence. Then in the fall, newly-arrived Moravian Philip Henry Molther began to teach a "stillness" doctrine based on Psalm 45:10 ("Be still, and know that I am God!"). This was the second of the two teachings of the Moravians in England that Wesley opposed, that one must not use means of grace such as the Lord's Supper, devotional reading of scripture, prayer, fasting, and doing

4. "A Short History of the People Called Methodists."

good to one's neighbor *until* one has a faith accompanied by an assurance that excludes doubt and one has, in effect, attained Christian perfection. Instead, one is to "be still," to wait for Christ apart from all means of grace, for to use the means of grace would be to trust in them, not in Christ.

This directly contradicted the practice of the Holy Club, and challenged Wesley's own Anglican tradition as well as his understanding of primitive Christianity. It set up sharp dichotomies between Christ and the means of grace he had ordained, and between grace and works. It would be hard to imagine a teaching that would so cut to the core of Wesley's fundamental commitments than the stillness doctrine.

The Wesley brothers contested this Moravian quietism in public and private but ultimately to no avail. In May, 1740, the Wesleys and their followers left Fetter Lane for good, bringing their group to join the Foundery Society which they had formed in April, and which made adherence to the means of grace one of its requirements for membership.[5]

MEDIATED IMMEDIACY[6]

The Fetter Lane controversy forced Wesley to further develop his understanding of grace and means of grace in critically important ways. The Moravian stillness teaching was arguing for the immediacy of grace apart from any means, denying that grace is mediated through certain practices ordained by Christ. To them the means of grace

---

5. This would also lead to their separation from their Holy Club colleagues who went with them to Georgia. Both Charles Delamontte and Benjamin Ingham would ally themselves with the Moravians.

6. I draw here on my earlier discussion in Knight, *Presence of God*, chapter 2.

were actually barriers to grace, works that diverted one from trusting in Christ.

But to fully grasp Wesley's theological response, we must examine how he was at the same time answering his critics from within his own Church of England. Rather than seeing Wesley as a proponent of salvation through works, as his Moravian opponents were prone to do, his Anglican detractors saw him as an "enthusiast," preaching an experiential gospel that was dangerously misleading. They instead recommended a religion that was both rational and moderate, using "rational" as the opposite of experiential.

To Wesley, this was "formalism," that is, having the form of godliness but not the power. For the formalist

> *religion* is commonly thought to consist of three things—harmlessness, using the means of grace, and doing good, that is, helping our neighbors, chiefly by giving alms. Accordingly by a "religious man" is commonly meant one that is honest, just, and fair in his dealings; that is constantly at church and Sacrament; and that gives much alms or (as it is usually termed) does much good.[7]

To this would sometimes be added an assent to basic Christian beliefs. This minimal belief, minimal morality, and dutiful church attendance was popularly considered all that was needed to attain a happy afterlife.

But Wesley was not only concerned with the next life but this life. One could do all of these things, he argued, and still lack the new life that God gives us in Christ. Christianity consists not of a minimal set of duties but holiness of heart and life. Writing in 1743, Wesley eloquently stated the governing motive of his Methodist movement:

---

7. "Journal 3," November 24, 1739, *Works* 11:45.

> We see on every side either men of no religion at all, or men of a lifeless, formal religion. We are grieved at the sight, and should greatly rejoice if by any means we might convince some that there is a better religion to be attained, a religion worthy of God that gave it. And this we conceive to be no other than love: the love of God and of all mankind; the loving God with all our heart and soul and strength, as having first loved *us*, as the fountain of all the good we have received, and of all we ever hope to enjoy; and the loving every soul which God hath made . . . as our own soul.[8]

"This is the religion," Wesley said, that "we long to see established in the world, a religion of love and joy and peace, having its seat in the heart, in the inmost soul, but ever showing itself by its fruit . . . spreading virtue and happiness all around it."[9]

Wesley thus found himself simultaneously rejecting the formalism he found in large segments of his own Church of England as well as the unmediated experientialism of the Moravian stillness teaching at Fetter Lane. In doing this Wesley was not simply calling for some sort of theological middle ground, but was challenging and ultimately transcending the assumed dichotomies that underlay the two positions.

First, he denied the dichotomy between reason and experience that was widely presupposed by eighteenth century scholars. The love, peace and joy he described in the heart are not passing feelings or sudden impulses, but settled dispositions that guide both our reasoning and our actions. Like his contemporary Jonathan Edwards, Wesley

---

8. "An Earnest Appeal to Men of Reason and Religion," ¶ 2, *Works* 11:45.

9. Ibid., ¶ 4, *Works* 11:46.

The Moravian Controversy

saw reason and experience not at war with one another but as integrated in human lives. We shall say more about this in chapter 6.

Second, he denied the dichotomy between immediate and mediated experience assumed by both formalism and the stillness teaching. In addressing formalist criticism of his talk of "immediate inspiration" by the Holy Spirit, and suggesting God only worked that way in apostolic times, Wesley responded:

> But all inspiration, though by means, is immediate. Suppose, for instance, you are employed in private prayer, and God pours his love into your heart. God then acts *immediately* on your soul; and the love of him which you then experience is as immediately breathed into you by the Holy Ghost as if you had lived seventeen hundred years ago. Change the term: say, God then *assists* you to love him? Well, and is not this immediate assistance? Say, His Spirit *concurs* with yours. You gain no ground. It is immediate concurrence, or none at all. God, a Spirit, acts upon your spirit.[10]

This response to formalism also contains within it Wesley's response to his opponents at Fetter Lane: though always immediate, inspiration is normally through means. Wesley readily agreed that to use means of grace such as prayer or the Lord's Supper without some degree of receptive faith is merely formalism, and ineffectual in advancing holiness. But when they are used with an open, receptive faith, they are the means by which we encounter the transforming presence of God. This understanding of a mediated immediacy in the means of grace, received by faith, became one

---

10. "A Farther Appeal to Men of Reason and Religion," Part I, ¶ V.28, *Works* 11:171–72.

of the most essential elements of Wesley's emerging theology and practice.

DISCUSSION QUESTIONS

1. What was the issue that split the Fetter Lane Society and why was it important?
2. What are "formalism" and "enthusiasm" and why did Wesley see them as dangers?
3. What is "mediated immediacy" and how does it respond to formalism and enthusiasm?

4

THE CALVINIST CONTROVERSY

THE AWAKENING BEGINS

It was in October 1738, not long after his return from Germany, that John Wesley read of a contemporary revival of the religion of the heart. The book was *A Faithful Narrative of the Surprising Work of God*, Jonathan Edward's account of the remarkable season of conversions at his Northampton parish in New England.[1] Here was an instance of the transforming work of the Holy Spirit on a large scale, bringing about occurrences in human lives similar to what had happened to Wesley at Aldersgate.

What Wesley may not have known at the time was that the Northampton revival was not unique. Similar events were occurring here and there on both sides of the Atlantic, most notably in Wales where since the 1720s Griffith

1. "Journal 3," October 10, 1738, *Works* 19:16.

Jones had been engaged in open air preaching. With the conversions of Daniel Rowland and Howell Harris in 1735, it would not be long before there would be a full-scale awakening in Wales.[2]

All this foreshadowed what was soon to come. The key figure in initiating the eighteenth century trans-Atlantic awakening was George Whitefield (1714–1770)[3] a friend of the Wesleys and one of the later participants in the Holy Club. Whitefield had been an aspiring actor until his conversion in 1735. While the Wesleys were enduring their time in Georgia, Whitefield's preaching in England began drawing large numbers of hearers. Although the newly returned John Wesley sought to dissuade him, Whitefield left for Georgia in early 1738. In America, as in England, his preaching the promise of new birth attracted large crowds. Back in England in 1739, Whitefield began preaching to thousands in Bristol. He had put his acting skills to good use in preaching the gospel, and his resulting popularity made him easily the best-known Methodist in England for at least a decade.

But Whitefield would soon leave for Wales, and then return to America, and wanted John Wesley to come to Bristol and continue the work he had begun. Wesley was not especially inclined to go, and the proposal that he should provoked lively discussion in the Fetter Lane Society. Coming to no conclusion after twelve days of discussion, Wesley wrote that "we at length all agreed to decide it by lots. And by this it was determined I should go."[4]

---

2. On the awakening in Wales see Jones et al., *Elect Methodists*, 11–14; and Rack, *Reasonable Enthusiast*, 222–26.

3. Biographies of Whitefield include Kidd, *George Whitefield*; Lambert, *"Pedlar in Divinity"*; and Stout *Divine Enthusiast*.

4. "Journal 3," March 28, 1738, *Works* 19:38.

The Calvinist Controversy

Wesley was concerned after he arrived when he discovered that Whitefield was preaching out of doors, which though not illegal was certainly irregular. "I could scarce reconcile myself at first to this *strange way* of preaching in the fields," Wesley wrote, "having been all my life (till very lately) so tenacious of every point relating to decency and order that I should have thought the saving of souls *almost a sin* if it had not been done *in a church*."[5] This "field preaching," as it was called, was not always or even often actually done in a field, but in a wide range of settings from the center of towns to mining pits.

Perhaps drawing comfort from preaching on the Sermon on the Mount the day before ("one pretty remarkable precedent of *field preaching*")[6], on April 2 Wesley "submitted to 'be more vile,' and proclaimed in the highways the glad tidings of salvation, speaking from a little eminence in a ground adjoining the city, to about three thousand people."[7] Wesley spent the rest of that month speaking both out of doors and to society meetings not held in churches, a pattern of ministry that would continue the rest of his life. By May, Charles Wesley was engaged in field preaching as well.

The irregularity of field preaching lay not only in its being outside a church building but that it was done without the permission of parish priests. Of course many clergy were opposed to Methodist preaching, but while they might keep it out of their pulpits it proved impossible to keep from their parishes. Wesley had been preaching to persons gathered in society meetings in various parishes even before he began field preaching, and was criticized for doing so. To the question "how is it that I assemble Christians who are

5. Ibid., March 29, 1738, *Works* 19:46.
6. Ibid., April 1, 1738.
7. Ibid., April 2, 1738.

none of my charge to sing psalms and pray and hear the scriptures expounded," Wesley responded, "I look upon *all the world as my parish*; thus far I mean, that in whatever part of it I am, I judge it meet, right, and my bounden duty to declare unto all that are willing to hear the glad tidings of salvation."[8]

Wesley was speaking for himself but he might as well have been speaking for all Methodists at the time. Itinerant preaching and the forming of societies apart from local parishes were characteristics that marked the Methodists and made them controversial, including with some evangelical Anglican priests who were otherwise supporters of the awakening. As we will see, opposition to the methods of the Methodists would become one of the impediments to greater unity among the various participants in the awakening.

FREE GRACE

The same month that John Wesley began field preaching he published his sermon, "Free Grace," to which was appended a hymn by Charles Wesley on "Universal Redemption." This was a full-scale attack on the Calvinist doctrine of predestination. Although Wesley requested that those who respond in opposition to this sermon do so "in charity, in love, and in the spirit of meekness,"[9] it must be said that Wesley's own language was emphatic: the doctrine of predestination tends "to overthrow the whole Christian revelation;"[10] it is, he said more than once, blasphemy, and represents "the

---

8. "Letter," March 28, 1739? *Works* 25:615–16.
9. "Free Grace," To the Reader, *Works* 3:544.
10. Ibid., ¶ 23, *Works* 3:554.

most high God . . . as more cruel, false, and unjust than the devil."[11]

These are strong words, and they predictably elicited a strong response. George Whitefield was decidedly Calvinist in his theology and wished Wesley had maintained public silence over their differences. But when Wesley persisted in preaching against predestination, Whitefield wrote a letter to Wesley not only defending predestination but attacking Wesley's understanding of the new birth and belief in Christian perfection. That letter became public in 1741, and a pamphlet war ensued.

While there was a measure of reconciliation between the Wesleys and Whitefield by the end of 1741, with expressions of mutual respect and personal affection all around, the unity of the awakening was now irreparably broken into Moravian, Calvinist and Wesleyan parts. The Wesleys two Georgia associates, Benjamin Ingham and Charles Delamotte, would join the Moravians. Whitefield, Howell Harris, and Daniel Rowland would be among the many who taught a Calvinist doctrine, and joined by two of John Wesley's more recent close associates, John Cennick and Joseph Humphries. All of this initially seemed to isolate Wesley from the mainstream, but it was not long before his movement would begin to flourish.

WESLEY'S ARMINIANISM[12]

Yet in 1739, as the conflicts with both Calvinism and the Moravian stillness doctrine were beginning, the future was anything but clear. We have seen how critical the issues were that led to the break with the Moravians. What were

---

11. Ibid., ¶ 25, *Works* 3:556.
12. For an in-depth exposition and analysis of Wesley's Arminianism, see McGonigle, *Sufficient Saving Grace*.

the issues that led Wesley to so publicly and directly challenge Calvinism?

To begin to answer this question, it should first be noted that in contrast to the Calvinists Wesley was a thoroughgoing Arminian, and had been so going back to his childhood. Wesley was not adopting a new theological position in 1739 but coming to a new understanding of its importance. What Wesley meant by the term "Arminian," which he uses as a self-designation later in his ministry, was much more precise that the usage common in his day. While it was used loosely to denote moralistic Anglicans, Arians, Deists, and advocates of human free will, Wesley's Arminianism was orthodox and evangelical—it was no accident he titled his sermon "Free Grace," not "Free Will." His theology was, in fact, quite close to the original.

That original was the theology of Jacob Arminius (1559–1609),[13] a Dutch Reformed theologian whose dissatisfaction with deterministic understandings of predestination and election led him to radically rethink their meaning. In this he faced strong opposition, but, as Rustin E. Brian notes, Arminius "risked everything—his career, his legacy, and his livelihood—to defend his fundamental impulse, namely, that all are elect in Christ, and thus have the real possibility of salvation. . . . God does not will that anyone should perish and be damned . . ."[14]

In challenging the traditional understanding of predestination, Arminius was not only questioning the teaching of John Calvin, but that of Martin Luther and Augustine as well. But it was Arminius' own Reformed tradition,

---

13. Biographies and theological analyses of Arminius include Brian, *Jacob Arminius*; Stanglin and McCall, *Jacob Arminius*; and Bangs, *Arminius*. An overview of the Arminian tradition can be found in Olson, *Arminian Theology*.

14. Brian, *Jacob Arminius*, 59.

The Calvinist Controversy

centered as it was on the sovereignty of God and divine grace, that was most in conflict with his proposal. Not long after his death, the Synod of Dort (1619) was convened to examine the issues raised by Arminius. The Synod rejected Arminianism and more precisely defined orthodox Calvinism. This definition is often summarized as "five-point Calvinism" or with the acronym TULIP, each letter of which stands for the beginning letter of each of the five points: Total depravity, Unconditional election, Limited atonement, Irresistible grace, and Perseverance of the Saints.

Neither Arminius nor Wesley would object to the first point, total depravity—the longest essay Wesley wrote was a vigorous defense of the doctrine of original sin in response to John Taylor's denial of it in the name of human free will and enlightened reason.[15] But both Arminius and Wesley would strongly reject the remaining four, all of which are implied by predestination. Unconditional election meant that one's election to salvation is totally determined by God, and there is nothing we need to do or can do that will affect our salvation one way or the other. Limited atonement held that Jesus Christ did not die for all humanity, but only for those who were predestined by God for election. Due to the irresistibility of grace, those who are among the elect would unfailingly receive justification and have faith, and once having salvation, that grace will prevent their falling away; hence the saints will persevere to the end.

This form of Calvinism, not Wesley's Arminianism, was the dominant theology of the eighteenth century awakening, although it could be found in more moderate or more extreme forms. Certainly the heritage of Puritanism partly lay behind its popularity. But it was also attractive because for many it provided a convincing explanation of

---

15. Wesley's essay on Original Sin can be found in *Works* 12:156–481.

their conversion experience, in which they as sinners felt overcome by the grace of God.

Wesley's objection to predestination was centered on three interrelated issues: what is the character of God, how does grace work, and what is the goal of salvation? His concern was pastoral as much as it was theological; that is, he believed the answers to these questions had a direct effect on how persons related to God and on what they sought and hoped for within that relationship.

We have already seen how in "Free Grace" Wesley charged predestinarians with blasphemy for their portrayal of God. The doctrine, he argued, represented Jesus Christ as a "hypocrite, a deceiver of the people," for while Jesus clearly "speaks *as if he was* willing that all men should be saved," predestination insisted "he did not *intend* to save all sinners." This was to describe Christ "as pretending the love which he had not."[16] As for God the Father, predestination "destroys all his attributes at once. It overturns both his justice, mercy and truth." How can God be just, Wesley asked, "when you say that God condemned millions of souls to everlasting fire . . . for continuing in sin, which for want of that grace *he will not* give, they cannot avoid."[17] When Calvinists said they could prove all this by scripture, Wesley insisted "No Scripture can mean that God is not love, or that his mercy is not over all his works."[18]

This really got to the heart of the matter for Wesley. The entirety of scripture—what he would call the whole tenor of scripture—attests to the love of God, and to interpret passages in a way that would overturn the whole was faulty exegesis. On a theological level, while respecting the freedom of God, Wesley simply denied the way

16. "Free Grace," ¶ 24, *Works* 3:554–55.
17. Ibid., ¶ 25, *Works* 3:555.
18. Ibid., ¶ 26, *Works* 3:556.

the Reformed tradition made the sovereignty of God the governing attribute. Commenting on I John 4:8 Wesley said "God is often styled holy, righteous, wise; but not holiness, righteousness, or wisdom . . . as He is said to be love; intimating that this is . . . His reigning attribute, the attribute that sheds an amiable glory on all His other perfections."[19] This was the bedrock upon which Wesley's theology rested. Moreover, he was convinced that our conception of God matters: how we live is definitively shaped by who we worship.

As a result of this understanding of God, Wesley took issue with the standard Calvinist description of how grace works. His central argument in "Free Grace" was for its universality—"free in all, and free for all"[20]—in contrast to the claim that grace was only given to the predestined elect. But in other writings Wesley also took direct aim at the Calvinist notion of grace as irresistible. If grace was both universal (as Wesley claimed) and irresistible (as the Calvinists held) then it would lead to universal salvation. But in accord with the Arminian tradition, Wesley argued that the initial work of grace (what he termed "prevenient" or "preventing" grace) was to restore in everyone a small measure of liberty to respond to God and a minimal moral conscience that convicts us by making us uneasy concerning our intentions and actions. It was only the restoration of liberty and conscience that was irresistible; for once restored we then had the capacity to respond or not to the continued reaching out to us by God. It was prevenient grace that enabled everyone to enter into a relationship with God, and it was this understanding of grace that enabled Wesley to affirm a Protestant version of original sin while denying predestination.

---

19. *Notes on the New Testament*, 1 John 4:8.
20. "Free Grace," ¶ 1, *Works* 3:545.

The third issue had to do with what grace can accomplish in this life. Wesley raised this in a preliminary way in "Free Grace" when he argued that predestination "tends to destroy Christian holiness, happiness, and good works . . ."[21] But what was at stake in his debate with the Calvinists was much more—it was the theological claim that governed Wesley's vision of divine salvation, that its purpose was to restore persons to the image of God in which they were created, and to do so in the present age. Calvinists simply denied Christian perfection was possible in this life. Part of the conflict was over the effect of grace—Calvinists emphasized grace as giving persons a new status before God, while Wesley emphasized grace as fundamentally transforming action by God. But it was also a difference in theological focus. Calvinists looked back to the cross and saw salvation as fully accomplished; Wesley saw the cross as the permanent foundation upon which the fullness of salvation would be accomplished in this life, through the work of the Holy Spirit. Although evident in his earlier post-Aldersgate writings, the future orientation of Wesley's theology would later become much more developed and explicit.

DISCUSSION QUESTIONS

1. Why was Wesley initially uncomfortable with "field preaching" and why did he finally embrace it?
2. Why did Wesley so strongly oppose predestination? How did the two sides in this controversy understand the nature of God and grace?
3. What is an Arminian?

---

21. Ibid., ¶ 19, *Works* 3:551.

5

PROCLAIMING THE WAY OF SALVATION

THE WESLEYAN CONNECTION

As THE METHODISTS DISTINGUISHED themselves from the Moravians while at the same time dividing into Calvinist and Wesleyan wings, the various itinerant preachers and societies began to affiliate with one leader or another. In the early 1740s, Calvinistic Methodist associations were established in Wales under the leadership of Daniel Rowland and Howell Harris, and in England by George Whitefield with the assistance of Harris and John Cennick.[1] Even more significant was the connection in England that was formed and directed by Selena, Countess of Huntingdon, beginning in the late 1760s and growing throughout the next

---

1. For more on this, see Jones, *Elect Methodists*, 54–63; and Rack, *Reasonable Enthusiast*, 282–84.

decade.[2] But by far the largest and most extensive was "Mr. Wesley's Connection."

It was in the 1740s and 1750s that Wesley greatly clarified and consolidated his theological emphases into a coherent way of salvation. He organized his societies to further their members' growth in salvation and faithfulness in mission. Wesley also assembled and deployed an increasing number of lay preachers to spread the message of salvation throughout the British Isles, especially in England. All of this would be controversial, but it would also prove to be highly effective.

Methodist societies, while serving in Pietist fashion as renewal groups within the larger church, were viewed with suspicion by many because they were overseen not by parish priests but persons like Whitefield or Wesley. The societies in connection with John Wesley were called the "United Societies," a name originally applied to the merger of two societies in London but then extended to all. Later in chapter 7 we will examine the societies and various subgroups within them.

But here we can examine Wesley's response to the criticism that his Methodists "divide the church." Given that a church consists of faithful people, Wesley asked how, according to the critics, do the Methodists divide the church? It is "by our societies.... We 'divide them' (you say) 'by uniting them together,'" that is, "we divide those who are thus united with each other from the rest of the church." This Wesley denied. Many in the societies continued coming to the Church for word and sacrament, and others who did not do so before now did. Moreover, Wesley said, it is "one of the fixed rules of our societies, that every member

---

2. For more on the Countess see Harding, *Countess of Huntingdon's Connexion* and *Selena, Countess of Huntingdon*; and Schlenther, *Queen of the Methodists*

attend the ordinances of God, i.e., that *he does not divide from the church*."[3]

Even more controversial was Wesley's use of lay preachers, who, like the Wesley brothers, traveled across parish boundaries and preached outside of church buildings, without the permission of local parish priests. Because his preachers acted solely under his direction, and not under the authority of a bishop or parish priest, their existence for many represented potential or actual schism from the Church. While a few priests actually welcomed Wesley's preachers in their parishes, the vast majority disapproved, including priests otherwise sympathetic to the awakening.

Much like field preaching itself, Wesley did not initially embrace having lay preachers. But the growth in the number of societies coupled with the loss of clergy allies due to his conflicts with the Calvinists led Wesley to turn to laity for leadership. Before leaving to join Whitefield, John Cennick and Joseph Humphries had begun preaching. Then in 1740, Thomas Maxfield began preaching at the Foundery society. As Adrian Burdon notes, Maxfield was the first of Wesley's "'Sons of the Gospel,' those converted to Christianity under the influence of John Wesley's preaching, to become an Assistant."[4] Maxfield had begun his preaching through divine guidance and without Wesley's permission; it was after hearing him that Wesley acknowledged his call. As the number of lay preachers grew, Wesley began assigning them annually to circuits. Wesley made the first circuit plan in 1754, with seven circuits; eventually there would be fifty.

Although John Wesley was emphatic that his unordained preachers lacked sacramental authority—a rule

---

3. "An Earnest Appeal to Men of Reason and Religion," ¶ 85, *Works* 11:82–83.

4. Burdon, *Authority and Order*, 23.

that several would violate—their irregularity and potential for schism was always more troubling to Charles Wesley. Though uneasily accepting lay preachers a practical necessity, Charles was a much stricter judge than John about who should be accepted into their ranks. Still, even Charles was willing to recognize an authentic calling by its fruits. But his overall negativity did not go unnoticed by the lay preachers, and created tension between the two brothers.[5]

In 1746, in response to the accusation that had done "a great deal of harm by breaking and setting aside order," Wesley asked "What is the end of all *ecclesiastical order?* Is it not to bring souls from the power of Satan to God? And to build them up in his fear and love? *Order*, then, is so far valuable as it answers these ends; and if it answers them not it is nothing worth."[6] The problem, said Wesley, was not the lack of order but lack "of the knowledge and love of God" that had kept so many in bondage.[7] The purpose of polity, then, was missional: did it further or hinder the work of God in the world?

Ryan Nicholas Danker describes Wesley's position this way, "Wesley never accepted the idea that the essence of the Church was in its 'forms'" but believed it "was found in its faithful proclamation of the Christian gospel." Rather than seeking to keep "the message within the Church, understood as its hierarchy and structure," as many otherwise sympathetic Anglican priests urged him to do, "Wesley saw all practical impediments to the spread of the gospel as a hindrance to the faith, and thus of the Church." As a result Wesley was enabled to "both maintain an irregular ministry and to insist that he was a faithful member of the Church of England because of his insistence that the essence of the

---

5. On this see Tyson, *Assist Me to Proclaim*, 186–98.
6. Ibid.
7. "Letter to John Smith," June 25, 1746, *Works* 26:205–6.

Proclaiming the Way of Salvation

Church of England was to be found in its teachings and not its practices."[8] Thus Wesley could write in 1789 "first, I will not separate from the Church; yet, in cases of necessity I will vary from it."[9]

Wesley's most extensive defense of his utilizing lay preachers and explanation of their role came late in his ministry, in the sermon just cited. By this time discontent with their status among Wesley's preachers had grown, and the sermon was not well-received. But as Albert Outler notes, the views here were consistent with Wesley's beliefs even prior to 1741, when Maxfield became his first lay assistant.[10]

In the sermon Wesley made two distinctions. First, he argued that in the Old Testament the office of prophet (with preaching authority) and priest (with sacramental authority) were separate, a pattern continued in the New Testament with the offices of evangelist and pastor. The two offices were only combined after Emperor Constantine became a Christian. Thus Wesley's lay preachers were prophets but not priests, and his use of them was another instance of his recovery of primitive Christianity. Second, Wesley distinguished between ordinary prophets who were educated in "schools of the prophets," and extraordinary prophets "on whom the Holy Ghost came in an extraordinary manner."[11] Wesley's preachers were "extraordinary messengers of the gospel in this latter sense."[12]

This concept of "extraordinary messengers" would prove useful to Wesley when he was faced with women who were called to preach. Having women preachers would take

8. Danker, *Wesley and the Anglicans*, 144–45.
9. "Prophets and Priests," ¶ 16, *Works* 4:81.
10. Ibid., Introductory Comments, *Works* 4:74.
11. Ibid., ¶ 6, *Works* 4:76–77.
12. Ibid., ¶ 11, *Works* 4:79.

Wesley's irregularities to a whole new level, so he was careful in his response to an inquiry from Sarah Crosby in 1761. Intending to lead a society meeting of around thirty people, she had found herself addressing two hundred, and what she did came very close to preaching. Wesley assured her, "I think you have not gone too far. You could not well do less." He advised her to tell the gathering "You lay me under great difficulty. The Methodists do not allow of women preachers. Neither do I take upon me any such character. But I will just nakedly tell you what is in my heart."[13] While some have seen this as a prohibition of her preaching, others have seen it as a permission as long as she did not call it preaching.[14] But one thing is clear: Wesley fully endorsed what she had done, and encouraged her to continue.

In any event, Sarah Crosby did undertake a preaching ministry, and her example encouraged other Methodist women to heed their calling as well. One of these was Mary Bonsanquet, who in 1771 sent Wesley an extensive defense of women's preaching understood as a response to an extraordinary call of God. In his reply Wesley was now prepared to unequivocally endorse women as lay preachers: "I think the strength of the cause rests there, on you having an *Extraordinary Call*. So, I am persuaded, has every one of our Lay Preachers . . ." As Methodism itself is "an extraordinary dispensation" of God, "I do not wonder if several things occur therein which do not fall under ordinary rules of discipline."[15] While never appointing a woman to a circuit, Wesley began providing women preachers with letters

---

13. "Letter to Sarah Crosby," February 14, 1761, *Works* 27:241–2.

14. Earl Kent Brown believes Wesley was permitting Crosby to testify and exhort but not to preach (*Women of Mr. Wesley's Methodism*, 26); Paul Wesley Chilcote argues Wesley was not prohibiting her from preaching (*Wesley and the Women Preachers*, 136n22).

15. Cited in Chilcote, *Wesley and the Women Preachers*, 122.

of endorsement, opening pulpits in Methodist chapels and other venues throughout the Wesleyan connection.

With an ever-growing body of preachers without formal theological training in the midst of a doctrinally diverse awakening, it became necessary to find ways to inform and guide their proclamation. Starting in 1748 Wesley had annual conferences to discuss questions around doctrine and discipline, both to sort out issues and to ensure those in connection with him were all on the same theological page. The minutes were first published in 1749, with significant revision in 1763, and were an essential resource for both teaching and practices for enabling Christian growth.

Even more important as a guide to doctrine were Wesley's *Sermons on Several Occasions*, three volumes of which were published between 1746 and 1750, with a fourth in 1760. Together with Wesley's *Explanatory Notes on the New Testament* (1755, with a revised edition in 1762) they became the doctrinal standards for Wesley's Methodists. During this same period Wesley also published his 50 volume *Christian Library* (1749-55) which was intended to provide his preachers with excerpts from a wide range of works on Christian spiritual practice and experience.

The result of all of this writing and publishing was to develop a carefully considered doctrine of Christian salvation with a corresponding set of spiritual practices. It was this doctrine his preachers were to proclaim, and this spiritual discipline they were charged to enforce.

UNIVERSAL GRACE

What, then, was this message of salvation that Wesley's preachers were to proclaim? At its heart it is the promise of recovery of the image of God (*imago Dei*) in which we were created. Both the atonement of Jesus Christ and the power of the Holy Spirit were the gracious work of God designed to bring about that restoration. Indeed, as we shall see, because of Christ we can be in the image of God more fully and completely than was possible for Adam and Eve.

Wesley described the image of God in which humanity was created in terms of three aspects or dimensions. The first, the "natural image," in turn consists of three capacities: understanding, liberty, and various affections or tempers. These affections or tempers[16] are the dispositions of the heart; they are the motivations and desires that direct the will. But because humans also have a capacity for liberty, they are free to deny their own dispositions and direct the will otherwise. This is what made the fall into sin possible, but it is also what enables persons to love in freedom, as God loves.

The second aspect is the "political image," which Wesley at times discussed explicitly and at other times implicitly. This is the human capacity to govern their world, mirroring God who is the governor of both heaven and earth. With this comes the responsibility to govern with the same love and justice as does God.

The third aspect is the most important, as it directly reflects the nature of God. The "moral image" is the original righteousness and holiness in which humanity was created. As God is love, so "man at his creation was full of love, which was the sole principle of all his tempers, thought, words, and actions."[17] This is humanity's "highest excellence" to be "a creature capable of God, capable of knowing, loving, and

---

16. There is disagreement among Wesley scholars concerning the relation of the terms "tempers" and "affections." Some like Gregory Scott Clapper, argue they are synonyms; others like Randy L. Maddox believe the affections are the onset of dispositions that, when they become habitual and enduring, are then called tempers. See Clapper, *John Wesley on Religious Affections*; Maddox, *Responsible Grace*, 69.

17. "The New Birth," ¶ I.1, *Works* 2:188.

obeying his Creator."[18] To be in the image of God is to have the capacity for such a relationship with God.

The fall of humanity into sin disrupted that relationship. Failing to continue to trust in God, humanity turned away from God and placed its trust in that which is other than God. As a result, this condition of a broken relationship with God leads to a consequent idolatry focused on ourselves and the world. The first step in restoring humanity to the image of God, then, is restoring a relationship with God.

This doctrine of original sin, which Wesley described as our (fallen) "natural state," is firmly Protestant in affirming total depravity, that is, the whole person is under this sinful condition. But it should be noted that Wesley came to reject the common Reformed belief that all persons are guilty of the sin of Adam and Eve. Wesley's later belief was that any such inherited guilt was universally negated by the atonement of Christ. We are responsible for our actual sins, whether inward or outward, and not for the sins of our original parents. Our problem is that we do inherit the sinful condition itself, and this inbred sin (or total corruption) in the heart leads to actual sin.

In this natural state, Wesley believed our fundamental problem is we do not know God. We can certainly infer from the created order that there is a God, but just as "we know there is an emperor of China, whom yet we do not know . . ."[19] so apart from grace we have no acquaintance with God. As we do not know God, we are unable to love God, and therefore delight in God.[20] Nor do we fear God:

---

18. "The General Deliverance," ¶ I.2., *Works* 2:439.
19. "Original Sin," ¶ II.3, *Works* 2:177.
20. Ibid., ¶ II.5, *Works* 2:178.

"we leave him to manage his own affairs, to sit quietly, as we imagine, in heaven, and leave us on earth to manage ours."[21]

Returning to the three dimensions of the image of God, we can see more clearly the impact of this broken relationship with God. The moral image is totally corrupted—our hearts and lives are not governed by love. With regard to the natural image, the disposition of the heart, or will, is now governed by unholy tempers, as characterized by sinful motivations and desires. The understanding is dimmed and more prone to error, and inclined to see the natural world as in effect the whole of reality. Without a relationship with God, our liberty vanishes, in that our choosing is now limited by our understanding and solely directed by an unholy will. As for the political image, our governance of the world is no longer marked by faithful stewardship on behalf of God, but by self-centeredness.

As we saw earlier, for Wesley no one in this natural state is devoid of grace. God reaches out to everyone through prevenient (or preventing) grace, which means "the grace that comes before." In one sense *all* grace is prevenient, in that it is all due to divine initiative. But in this more particular form, prevenient grace refers to the work of God in all persons designed to create an awareness of their condition and to draw them back to God.

The primary work of prevenient grace is twofold. First, within the understanding the Holy Spirit creates in everyone a conscience, which, said Wesley, "in one sense may be termed 'natural', because it is found in all men, yet properly speaking it is not *natural*; but a supernatural gift of God..." Though this universal conscience only provides a general sense of right and wrong, and not the fullness of the law of God, even that is from the Son of God who enlightens everyone in the world (John 1:9). "And," Wesley continued, "it

---

21. Ibid., ¶ II.6, *Works* 2:178.

is his Spirit who giveth thee an inward check, who causeth thee to feel uneasy, when thou walkest in any instance contrary to the light which he hath given thee."[22] Second, prevenient grace restores a measure of liberty, enabling us to respond to God, whether through obeying our conscience or to receiving further light through hearing the message of the gospel. Thus salvation for Wesley begins here, with "the first wish to please God, the first dawn of light concerning his will, and the first slight, transient conviction of having sinned against him. All these imply some tendency toward life, some degree of salvation . . . ."[23]

KNOWING GOD

Following this description of prevenient grace, in one of his most succinct summations, Wesley lays out the remainder of the way of salvation:

> Salvation is carried on by 'convincing grace', usually in Scripture termed 'repentance', which brings a larger measure of self-knowledge, and a further deliverance from the heart of stone. Afterwards we experience the proper Christian salvation, whereby 'through grace' we 'are saved by faith', consisting of two grand branches, justification and sanctification. By justification we are saved from the guilt of sin, and restored to the favour of God; by sanctification we are saved from the power and root of sin, and restored to the image of God.[24]

In itself, prevenient grace provides for a minimal morality and a slight intimation of God, thus already bringing

---

22. "On Conscience," ¶ 5, *Works* 3:482.
23. "On Working Out Our Own Salvation," ¶ II. 1, *Works* 3:202–4.
24. Ibid., *Works* 204.

to persons a small measure of salvation. But the purpose of prevenient grace is fundamentally to prepare people to hear the gospel and enable their response.

Although the gospel is good news, the initial effect of hearing it is to awaken sinners, convicting them of their sins. While before they had an uneasy conscience, this convincing work of grace enables them to measure their lives against God's moral law, and more clearly see their fallen condition. As a result they now see themselves as under the judgment of God.

Because the moral law is itself a picture of God's righteousness, it also reflects the original righteousness of humanity created in God's image, before the fall into sin. While Wesley agreed with many other Protestants in looking to the Ten Commandments for the content of the law, he also emphasized Jesus' teachings, especially in the Sermon on the Mount, and declaring the two greatest commandments (Matthew 22:34–40) as absolutely central to God's law. In so doing, Wesley redirected attention from simply focusing on outward sin to the inward disposition of the heart, and from focusing on the written law to Christ as the embodiment of the law.

This knowledge of the law produces a greater self-knowledge which for Wesley was the heart of repentance. "The Holy Spirit," he said, "prepares us for his inward kingdom by removing the veil from our heart, and enabling us to know ourselves as we are known of him; by convincing us of sin . . ."[25] Those so convicted "feel themselves at once altogether guilty and altogether helpless."[26] The guilt is not so much a subjective feeling—we know of persons who feel guilty but should not, and others who should feel guilty but

---

25. "On the Discoveries of Faith," ¶ 12, *Works* 4:34.
26. Ibid., *Works* 435.

do not. This is instead an objective state, a stark recognition that we stand before God as sinners.

Accompanying guilt is a sense of helplessness. While we strive to do good, we become ever more aware of the deep hold sin has over our hearts and lives, and our inability on our own to conquer it. This directs us to God as our only hope for forgiveness and a new life.

Repentance, then, is itself a gradual work of God that takes place over time. An extensive study by Tom Albin has shown that Wesley's Methodists spent an average of 2.3 years being nurtured through the spiritual disciplines and small groups of the Methodist movement prior to experiencing a new birth, while only a quarter experienced new birth as the direct result of preaching.[27] This is in sharp contrast to most nineteenth century revivalists, who taught that God was only waiting on our decision to forgive our sins and renew our hearts. Wesley did not know why God works in different ways in different lives. There are, he said, "a thousand circumstances that attended the process of our conviction that we do not understand. We know not why he suffered us to stay so long before he revealed his Son in our hearts; or why this change from darkness to light was accompanied with such and such particular power. And we cannot give any reason why of two persons equally athirst for salvation one is presently taken into the favour of God and the other left to mourn for months or years."[28] What we do know is that, in God's own way and timing, God will fulfill the promise, and awaken sinners "athirst for salvation" who wait for the promised blessing with an expectant yet patient faith.

---

27. Cited in Runyon, *New Creation*, 115.

28. "The Imperfection of Human Knowledge," ¶ III 3–4, *Works* 2:583–84.

This means that while persons undergoing repentance lack the full Christian faith (the faith of a child of God), neither are they without faith. As Wesley noted, "this conviction implies a species of faith," the "faith of a servant." If the fundamental condition of the fall into sin was a broken relationship such that persons no longer know or love God, the faith of a servant effects a partial restoration of a conscious relationship with God through enabling a partial knowledge of God. Those who have this faith now have knowledge "of the *invisible* and *eternal* world"; they both fear God and work righteousness. Although they have not yet received forgiveness of their sins through justification, they are nonetheless accepted by God,[29] and should they die in this state will be with God in paradise.

Wesley came to this understanding of the faith of a servant later in his ministry, and in the 1770s began amending his description of his spiritual state prior to Aldersgate with notations like "I certainly then had the faith of a *servant*, though not the faith of a son."[30] He had come to realize that before Aldersgate he did have a conscious and living relationship with God, albeit one governed by fear of God rather than love.

Stanley J. Rodes has drawn attention to the larger covenantal structure which frames this twofold understanding of faith. Rodes argues that the Puritans bequeathed to the larger English theological world a Reformed covenant of works for the non-elect, based on obeying the law given to Adam and Moses; and a Covenant of Grace for the elect grounded in Jesus Christ. The elect are thus saved through Christ's obedience in fulfilling the law.

Wesley's Arminian revision limits the Covenant of Works to Adam prior to the Fall (an age of innocence) and

29. "On the Discoveries of Faith," ¶ 12–13, *Works* 4:35.
30. "Journal," April 25, 1738, *Works* 18:235.

extends the Covenant of Grace to encompass all humanity after the fall (the loss of innocence). Within the Covenant of Grace are two dispensations: the Legal Dispensation related to Moses, prior to the outpouring of the Holy Spirit; and the Evangelical Dispensation grounded in Christ, inaugurated by the outpouring of the Holy Spirit at Pentecost. Those with the faith of a servant are responding to grace in terms of the Legal Dispensation; those with the faith of a child of God to grace in terms of the Evangelical Dispensation.[31] What is central to Wesley's theological vision is that *both* the law and the gospel are gifts of grace, both are aspects of the way of salvation, but it is only with the coming of Christ and outpouring of the Spirit that hearts can be changed and new life received.

It is justification and the new birth in which love begins to govern our relationship with God, and as we have seen these are received through faith in Jesus Christ. Taken together, they are an instantaneous and transformative work of God, the product of divine agency that is received by a repentant heart.

Although they occur together in an instant, within Wesley's theology faith is the logical precondition of justification, and justification for new birth and sanctification. It is faith that fully restores the broken relationship with God by enabling us to know and love God. Wesley argued that "without faith we cannot be . . . saved. For we can't rightly serve God unless we love him; And we can't love him unless we know him; neither can we know God, unless by faith."[32]

The Moravians had convinced Wesley that he needed faith, understood as trusting in Jesus Christ for salvation,

---

31. For the full argument see Rodes, *From Faith to Faith*, especially chapters 2–4.

32. "A Farther Appeal to Men of Reason and Religion," I, ¶ I.3, *Works* 11:106.

what Wesley came to call the faith of a child of God. But Wesley soon began to argue that our ability to trust and love God is itself dependent on faith enabling us to *know* God, by which he meant not simply knowledge in the sense of having reliable information, but knowing God in a way analogous to how persons know one another. Through faith, Wesley said, we have "a true spiritual acquaintance with him."[33]

Drawing on Hebrews 11:1, Wesley described faith as "the demonstrative evidence of things unseen, the supernatural evidence of things invisible, not perceivable by eyes of flesh, or by any of our natural senses or faculties." It is "that divine evidence whereby the spiritual man discerneth God and the things of God." Faith is thus analogous to our five senses; it "is with regard to the spiritual world what sense is with regard to the natural."[34] Wesley communicated this understanding of faith with a range of imagery. Faith is, he said, "the eye of the new born soul" enabling us to see the invisible God, or "the ear of the soul" whereby we hear the voice of God" speaking forgiveness.[35] Faith is what "draws aside the veil which hangs between mortal and immortal being."[36]

This description of faith as a "spiritual sense" is applied both to the faith of a servant and the faith of a child of God. But while those with the faith of a servant are convinced of their sins and struggle to obey God out of fear of God, those with the faith of a child of God know the love of Christ and their obedience is in response to that love.

33. Ibid.

34. "An Earnest Appeal to Men of Reason and Religion," ¶ 6, *Works* 116.

35. Ibid., ¶ 7, *Works* 11:46–47.

36. "On the Discoveries of Faith," ¶ 8, *Works* 4:32.

Proclaiming the Way of Salvation

This "invisible" or "spiritual" world which faith enables us to know has past, future, and present dimensions. The death of Jesus Christ on a cross is a past event, but through faith it becomes more than an account of a first century event—we experience its reality and it affects our hearts and lives. Likewise the return of Jesus and the establishing of his kingdom is yet to come, but through faith we experience in the present this future reality. Then there is the present activity of the Holy Spirit, invisible to our five senses, but discernable through faith. Thus faith transcends the barriers of time as well as the limitations of materiality, and opens us to encounter and be transformed by the "unseen" things of God.

Although occurring together, the faith of a child of God is the logically necessary precondition for justification. Wesley defined justification, according to the "plain scriptural notion," as "pardon, the forgiveness of sins." It is the "act of God the Father whereby," for the sake of the atonement of God the Son, we receive remission of sins.[37] "Justifying faith" therefore "implies, not only a divine evidence or conviction that 'God was in Christ, reconciling the world to himself', but a sure trust and confidence that Christ died for my sins, that he loved *me*."[38] It is at the time one believes this that one is justified.

Intrinsic to this faith is an assurance, given through the witness of the Spirit. Drawing on Romans 8:16, which he translated as "the Spirit itself beareth witness with our spirit, that we are children of God,"[39] Wesley argued that we can neither love nor trust God until we first know that God has loved and accepted us. This we know through the witness of the Spirit, "an inward impression on the soul,

37. "Justification by Faith," ¶ II.5, *Works* 189.
38. Ibid., ¶ IV.2, *Works* 1:194.
39. "The Witness of the Spirit I," *Works* 1:269.

whereby the Spirit of God directly 'witnesses to my spirit that I am a child of God'; that Jesus Christ hath loved me, and given himself for me; that all my sins are blotted out, and I, even I, am reconciled to God."[40]

Forgiveness and reconciliation fundamentally alters our relationship with God. It lays a new foundation in the heart, in which fear of God begins to be replaced by love for God as our governing motivation and disposition. In this way justification is logically prior to the new birth, which begins sanctification. While both occur together, Wesley said, "in order of thinking . . . justification precedes the new birth. We first conceive his wrath to be turned away, and then his Spirit to work in our hearts."[41]

To know God in this way—as having loved us even unto death on a cross—and to thereby be reconciled to God through the forgiveness of our sins, is to enter a new life. It was this promise that Wesley's preachers were called to proclaim; and it was to help persons attain that promise for which Wesley's societies were organized.

DISCUSSION QUESTIONS

1. What were some of the key characteristics of Wesley's "Connection" and why were they so controversial?
2. According to Wesley, what does it mean to be in the image of God?
3. What is prevenient grace, and what is its effect?
4. How do we know God?
5. What is the difference between having the "faith of a servant" and the "faith of a child of God"?

---

40. Ibid., ¶ I.7, *Works* 1:274.
41. "The New Birth," par. 1, *Works* 2:187.

6

RESTORING THE IMAGE OF GOD

THE NEW BIRTH

"Our main doctrines," wrote Wesley, "which include all the rest, are three, that of repentance, of faith, and of holiness. The first of these we account, as it were, the porch of religion; the next, the door; the third is religion itself."[1] This image needs some nuance in light of Wesley's mature theology: repentance is enabled by the faith of a servant, and, as we shall see, Wesley also spoke of the repentance of believers. Nonetheless, its central point governed Wesley's theology from the beginning of his ministry until the end: the goal of salvation is not forgiveness but holiness, not justification but sanctification; salvation is to be restored to the

---

1. "The Principles of a Methodist Father Explained," ¶ VI.4, *Works* 9:227.

image of God in this life. The beginning of that sanctification, that restoration, is the new birth.

Wesley described the new birth as "that great change which God works in the soul when he brings it into life: when he raises it from the death of sin to the life of righteousness. It is the change wrought in the whole soul by the almighty Spirit of God when it is 'created anew in Christ Jesus', when it is 'renewed after the image of God' . . . when the love of the world is changed into the love of God . . ."[2] The emphasis here is on divine agency, a transformative work of God which gives one a new heart and enables one to enter into a new life.

Wesley drew a sharp distinction between justification and the new birth (also called regeneration). Although they "are in point of time inseparable from each other," according to Wesley, they are

> things of a widely different nature. Justification implies only a relative change, the new birth a real change. God in justifying us does something for us; in begetting us again he does the work *in* us. . . . The one restores us to the favour of God, the other to the image of God. The one is taking away the guilt, the other taking away the power, of sin.[3]

Justification, then, has to do with placing us in a new relationship with God (the "relative change") through forgiveness of sins and the restoration to God's favor. The new birth is an actual transformation of the heart in which the power of sin—the hold sin has over our lives through original sin—is broken. Sin remains, but now it no longer

---

2. "The New Birth," ¶ II.5, *Works* 2:193–94.

3. "The Great Privilege of Those That Are Born of God," ¶ 2, *Works* 1:431–32.

reigns; indeed it can be conquered by the new principle of love inscribed in our hearts by the Holy Spirit.

Wesley further clarified the relation of justification and the new birth (and sanctification) in his discussion of the "imputed righteousness of Christ." This was a term beloved by some of his Calvinist critics, but not one Wesley insisted upon as it is not found in scripture. Although cautious in using the phrase due to prevalent misunderstanding, Wesley did not object to it if it was properly defined. For Wesley, the righteousness of Christ was imputed to believers in that they "are forgiven and accepted, not for the sake of anything in them or of anything that ever was, that is, or ever can be done by them, but wholly and solely for the sake of what Christ hath done and suffered for them."[4] To receive this righteousness we must repent, for until we "cast away all confidence in our own righteousness . . . we cannot have a true confidence in his."[5] Thus imputed righteousness is the ground of justification.

What Wesley firmly rejected was linking imputed righteousness to new birth and sanctification. What we fear, said Wesley, is that someone "should use the phrase 'righteousness of Christ', or, 'the righteousness of Christ is "imputed to me,"' as a cover for his unrighteousness."[6] The fear was not unfounded. There were elements in the awakening, especially among the Calvinists, who were convinced their own righteousness was irrelevant to their salvation since they were clothed with that of Christ. This antinomianism completely undercut the purpose of salvation, which is our restoration to the image of God through receiving a new life in Christ.

---

4. "The Lord Our Righteousness," ¶ II.5, *Works* 1:455.
5. Ibid., ¶ II.11, *Works* 1:458.
6. Ibid., ¶ II.19, *Works* 1:462.

Such teaching was the unintended consequence of language going back to the Protestant reformers. Wesley was clear in his rejection of it: God is not "*deceived* in those whom he justifies; that he thinks them to be in fact what they are not, that he accounts them to be otherwise than they are."[7] Justification consists of forgiveness, acceptance and reconciliation, but does not imply that when God looks upon us God now sees us as actually righteous even though we are in reality still sinners. No, said Wesley, "God *implants* righteousness in every one to whom he has *imputed* it."[8] This implanted righteousness begins with the new birth.

In addition to distinguishing the new birth from justification, Wesley also distinguished it from sanctification. While sanctification is "a progressive work carried on in the soul by slow degrees," this is not true of the new birth. While the new birth "is a part of sanctification" it is "not the whole; it is the gate of it, the entrance to it. When we are born again, then our sanctification, our inward and outward holiness, begins."[9]

In its full extent, holiness is "no less than the image of God stamped upon the heart. It is no other than the whole mind that was in Christ. It consists of all heavenly affections and tempers mingled together in one."[10] The heart of holiness is gratitude to God and benevolence to others.[11]

The new birth is our entry into this life at its inception. Through it, Wesley said, we "are inwardly renewed by the power of God. We feel the 'love of God shed abroad in our heart by the Holy Ghost which given unto us', producing

---

7. "Justification by Faith," ¶ II.4, *Works* 1:188.
8. "The Lord Our Righteousness," ¶ II.12, *Works* 1:458.
9. "The New Birth," ¶ IV.3, *Works* 2:198.
10. Ibid., ¶ III.1, *Works* 2:194.
11. "The Unity of the Divine Being," ¶ 16, *Works* 4:66–67.

love to all mankind . . ."[12] The focus is resolutely on the changed heart. It is holiness of heart that leads to holiness of life; indeed without a change of heart a holy life that mirrors the image of God is not possible.

As we have seen, for Wesley, "true religion, in the very essence of it, is nothing short of *holy tempers*."[13] These holy tempers are not feelings that come and go but abiding dispositions that make us the kind of persons we are. They are akin to what Paul calls fruit of the Spirit. They govern our intentions and desires, and provide the motivations for our actions. The primary holy tempers are faith, hope, and especially love, both for God and one's neighbors.

But while these holy tempers are dispositions in the heart, created and shaped by the Holy Spirit, they are intrinsically relational in that they are directed toward objects. We don't just have faith, but faith is always *in* something or someone; we don't just love but always love something or someone. Moreover, who or what we love determines the content of the temper. To love money, power, or fame is quite different from loving God; only the latter is a *holy* temper, and each love leads to a different way of life. For Wesley it also matters *which* God we love—a holy temper in the Christian sense is to love the God revealed in Jesus Christ. It is God's love *in Christ* that we are meant to image in our own hearts and lives.

Hence Wesley's description of the Christian life, from new birth on, is christocentric in two senses. First, it is a *response* to God's love for us in Christ, and marked by gratitude and praise. This in turn provides the ability and desire to *imitate* Christ, that is, to love as Christ loves, which the Holy Spirit enables us to do. This also means that we only retain this new life through continuing to be in relationship

12. "The Scripture Way of Salvation," ¶ I.4, *Works* 2:158.
13. "On Charity," ¶ 12, *Works* 3:306.

with God. The holy tempers are a reality in the heart that make us who we are, but to turn away from God is to become a different person in both heart and life. As we will see, much of the structure of Wesley's societies was designed to aid persons in remaining in a relationship with God.

In addition to holiness, the new birth is also the inception of happiness. Wesley was convinced that "except he be born again none can be happy even in this world," as "it is not possible in the nature of things that a man should be happy who is not holy." This is because "all unholy tempers are uneasy tempers. Not only malice, hatred, envy, jealously, revenge, create a present hell in the breast, but even the softer passions, if not kept within due bounds, give a thousand times more pain than pleasure." As long as these sources of sin "reign in any soul happiness has no place there. But they must reign till the bent of our nature is changed, that is, till we are born again."[14]

The fundamental reason unholy tempers cannot produce happiness is when they govern our hearts we are not the persons we were created to be. It is not "the happiness for which we were made." This happiness begins with justification and the new birth. As Wesley explained,

> We are happy, first, in the consciousness of his favour, which is indeed better than life itself; next, in the constant communion with the Father, and with his Son, Jesus Christ; then in all the heavenly tempers which he hath wrought in us by his Spirit; again, in the testimony of his Spirit that all our works please him; and lastly, in the testimony of our own spirit . . ."[15]

---

14. "The New Birth," ¶ III.3, *Works* 2:195–96.
15. "The Unity of the Divine Being," ¶ 17, *Works* 4:67.

There is happiness in once again being in the relationship with God for which we were created, and to be persons who once again reflect the image of God. And as we grow in holiness, we likewise grow in happiness.

"From the time of our being 'born again,'" Wesley said, "the gradual work of sanctification takes place." As "we are more and more dead to sin," that is, as our unholy desires and motivations decrease, "we are more and more alive to God," as holy tempers increasingly govern our hearts and lives.[16] While in the new birth the power of sin is broken it is still present in the heart; "it does not *reign*," said Wesley, "but it does *remain*."[17] Wesley believed that persons now no longer commit known outward sin, but they nonetheless struggle with intentional sin in the heart. The purpose of sanctification is to eliminate intentional sin over time, and replace it with love and other accompanying holy tempers.

Given that intentional sin remains, the process of sanctification necessarily includes what Wesley called the "repentance of believers." There is, he said, "a repentance consequent upon, as well as a repentance previous to justification." The repentance following justification" is widely different from that which is antecedent to it," in that it "implies no guilt, no sense of condemnation," nor does it "doubt the favour of God." Recalling that repentance is at heart a form of self-knowledge, the repentance of believers is "a conviction wrought by the Holy Ghost" of the sin remaining in the heart, and cleaving to our words and actions.[18]

We can also see in this that, while human responsiveness in the form of repentance and faith is necessary for growth in sanctification, that response itself is enabled by the Holy Spirit. Indeed, the whole of sanctification is a

16. "The Scripture Way of Salvation," ¶ I.8, *Works* 2:160.
17. "The Repentance of Believers," ¶ I.2, *Works* 1.337.
18. "The Scripture Way of Salvation," ¶ III. 5–6, *Works* 2:164–65.

creative act of God, in which love and all other holy tempers increasingly fill and govern the heart.

CHRISTIAN PERFECTION

Thus growing in sanctification, Wesley said, "we wait for entire sanctification, for a full salvation from our sins, from pride, self-will, anger, unbelief, or, as the Apostle expresses it, 'Go on to perfection.'" Christian perfection "means perfect love. It is love excluding sin; love filling the heart, taking up the whole capacity of the soul."[19]

As has been said, this was the most distinctive and controversial teaching of John Wesley. Wesley insisted upon Christian perfection in this life as the purpose of salvation, the goal of God's redemptive work in Jesus Christ and through the Holy Spirit. It was, he wrote in 1790, near the end of his life, the primary reason for the existence of Methodism: "This doctrine is the grand depositum which God has lodged with the people called Methodists; and for the sake of propagating this chiefly He appears to have raised us up."[20]

Besides his central claim that God seeks to restore us to the image of God in this life, Wesley found himself responding to controversy about the manner and timing of Christian perfection, as well as having to clear up misunderstandings within and without his movement over its content. With regard to the manner, Wesley's mature position (in 1767) was that "perfection is always wrought in the soul buy a simple act of faith; consequently, in an instant. But I believe a gradual work, both preceding and following

---

19. Ibid., ¶ I.9, *Works* 2:160.
20. "Letter to Robert C. Blackenberry," September 15, 1790, *Works* (J) 13:9.

that instant."[21] That is, he was thinking of it in a way parallel to the new birth. It is instantaneous, but like the new birth preceded and followed by a gradual work.

With regard to the time, Wesley believed "this instant generally is the instant of death, the moment before the soul leaves the body. But I believe it may be ten, twenty, or forty years before."[22] Because it is a work of God, it occurs at God's timing. So while one should not despair at not having received it, one can still look for it with expectant faith, and that very yearning will at the minimum spur on the gradual work of sanctification.

But the greatest difficulty Wesley faced was in defining "perfection." Part of the problem is that the word in English is derived from a Latin root that defines perfection as absolute, finished, and thus with no room to improve. But the Greek word used in the New Testament and by primitive Christianity does not mean an absolute perfection but perfection in terms of reaching a particular goal. It means something more like full grown or mature—when a child reaches adulthood he or she is perfected in terms of that goal, adulthood. The goal of Christian perfection is to be restored to the image of God; perfection is reached when that goal is attained.

Thus Wesley insisted, "Absolute perfection belongs not to man, nor to angels, but to God alone."[23] Neither can we attain angelic perfection or the perfection of Adam before his fall into sin. Unlike them, we are liable to mistakes.[24] Therefore

---

21. "Brief Thoughts on Christian Perfection," ¶ 2, *Works* 13:199.

22. Ibid., ¶ 3.

23. "A Plain Account of Christian Perfection," ¶ 2.6, *Works* 13:187.

24. "On Perfection," ¶ 2:1–2, *Works* 3:72–73.

> the highest perfection which man can attain while the soul dwells in the body does not exclude ignorance and error and a thousand other infirmities. Now from wrong judgments wrong words and actions will often necessarily flow.... I may think more or less of you than I ought to think.... And this mistake in my judgment may not only occasion something wrong in my behaviour, but it may still have a deeper effect—it may occasion something wrong in my affection.[25]

Here Wesley made a distinction that most of the Protestant reformers did not. For them, sin was whatever was in violation of the perfect will of God. But Wesley distinguished between "*sin properly so called*, that is, a voluntary transgression of a known law," and sin "improperly so called, that is, an involuntary transgression of a divine law, known or unknown ..." While both need "the atoning blood" for forgiveness, Wesley believed "there is no such perfection in this life as excludes these involuntary transgressions, which I apprehend to be naturally consequent on the ignorance and mistakes inseparable from mortality."[26] This means, among other things, that those who attain Christian perfection continue to pray for forgiveness.

Wesley also believed Christian perfection did not make one immune from temptation. This is a reversal of his earlier view in 1740 that Christian perfection did deliver persons from being susceptible to temptation.[27] But given the understanding that Christian perfection restores to the image of God which Adam and Eve possessed prior to the fall, there would be no grounds to claim that a person who

---

25. Ibid., ¶ I.3, *Works* 3:73.
26. "A Plain Account of Christian Perfection," ¶ 19, *Works* 13:169–70.
27. Ibid., ¶ 13, *Works* 13:151.

has that image could no longer yield to temptation, as that is what Adam and Eve did. Thus Wesley said in 1767, "I do not include an impossibility of falling from it, either in part or in whole," and retracted some earlier statements that said otherwise.[28] The central cause of falling is not the sin itself but the turning from God to the tempter, and placing our trust there, which is the precondition of sin.

While it is important to say what perfection is not, even more crucial is stating with clarity what it is. One of Wesley's most succinct definitions was in a letter he wrote in 1771: "Entire sanctification, or Christian perfection, is neither more nor less than pure love; love expelling sin, and governing the heart and life of a child of God."[29] Love for God, accompanied by love for neighbor and all other holy tempers, now fills the heart and becomes our motivations and desires. This holiness of heart leads to holiness of life; we have the mind that was in Christ and therefore walk as Christ walked. Having the mind of Christ "immediately and directly refers to the humility of our Lord," but has "a far more extensive sense, so as to include that whole disposition of his mind, all his tempers, both toward God and man."[30]

To be restored to the image of God is to be made in the image of the humanity of Jesus Christ, to love as he loved and to live as he lived. Yet this is even more than a restoration. We have seen how, in one sense, Christian perfection does not attain Adamic perfection, as we continue to have bodily infirmities and dimmed understanding, leading to mistakes in judgment and actions. But there is also a sense in which Christian perfection *exceeds* Adamic perfection, and this is due to the cross of Jesus Christ.

---

28. "Brief Thoughts on Christian Perfection," ¶ 1, *Works* 13:199.

29. "Letter to Walter Churchey," February 21, 1771, *Works* (J) 12:432.

30. "On Perfection," ¶ I.5, *Works* 3:74.

Wesley argued that "by the fall of Adam" humanity has gained "a capacity of attaining more holiness and happiness on earth than it would be possible to attain if Adam had not fallen. For if Adam had not fallen Christ had not died." Thus, without the fall "there would have been no room for that amazing display of God's love to mankind"[31] The consequence of this is that, while there could be faith in God, there could be no faith in the Father giving his only Son out of love for us, in the Son giving himself out of love for us, or in the Holy Spirit "raising us from the death of sin to the life of righteousness."[32] Nor could we love the triune God in response to God's love for us. "The chief ground of this love," said Wesley, "is plainly declared by the Apostle: 'We love him, because he first loved us.' But the greatest instance of his love had never been given if Adam had not fallen."[33]

To be restored to the image of God, then, is not merely the recovery of what was lost. It is to love as God has loved us, in response to and in imitation of the fullness of God's love for us in the cross of Jesus Christ. Thus Christian perfection is ultimately eschatological: it is the life of the Kingdom of heaven already present in the hearts and lives of believers, an anticipation of the future even more than a return to the past, because that Kingdom itself is filled and governed by God's love as manifested in Jesus Christ.

GROWING IN PERFECTION

Wesley has said that Christian perfection was not only preceded but followed by a gradual work of God. Those who attain Christian perfection earlier than their time of death should expect and enjoy continued growth. Much as new

---

31. "God's Love to Fallen Man," ¶ I.1, *Works* 2:425–26.
32. Ibid., ¶ I.2, *Works* 2:426.
33. Ibid., ¶ I.4, *Works* 2:427.

birth was a new foundation in one's life provided by the Holy Spirit to enable sanctification; so Christian perfection provides a foundation for growth in perfection.

So what does this growth entail? First, there is an intensified dependence on Christ. "None feel their need of Christ like these"; Wesley wrote, "none so entirely depend upon him. For Christ does not give life to the soul separate from, but in and with himself."[34] There is a crucial point being made in that second sentence that applies to the entire process of sanctification and perfection. We have this life, these holy tempers, only insofar as we are participating in a relationship with Jesus Christ. They are indeed "us," they are who we are, but we can only have a new life in Christ if we are dependent on and responding to Christ.

Second, we seek to overcome all limits to our living out this love faithfully and effectively. This means improving our knowledge and understanding so that our judgments and actions more accurately effect what we intend. We are increasingly learning *how* to love.

Third, the presence of involuntary transgressions necessitates continued repentance. There are "no persons living," wrote Wesley, who are so deeply conscious of their needing Christ both as prophet, priest, and king as those who believe themselves, and whom I believe, to be cleansed from all sin . . ." They are conscious of not only "their own ignorance" but also their "littleness of grace, coming short of the full mind that was in Christ, and walking less [accurately] than they might have done after their divine pattern . . ."[35] Thus those who attain Christian perfection continue

---

34. "A Plain Account of Christian Perfection," ¶ 9, Q. [5]. *Works* 13:169.

35. "Letter to the Rev. Samuel Furly," September 15, 1762, *Works* 27:302.

to pray for forgiveness as they also seek to grow in their ability to enact love in the world.

Consequently, Wesley insisted it is not a contradiction to say that there is no perfection "which does not admit of a continual increase. So that how much soever any man has attained, or in how high a degree soever he is perfect, he hath still need to 'grow in grace', and daily to advance in the knowledge of God his Saviour."[36] Wesley's advice to those who "have attained a measure of perfect love" is applicable to persons at any point along the way of salvation. When God has "enabled you to love with all your heart and with all your soul, think not of resting there. That is impossible. You cannot stand still; you must either rise or fall. . . . Therefore the voice of God to . . . the children of God is, 'Go forward.'"[37]

DISCUSSION QUESTIONS

1. What is the "new birth" and how does it differ from justification?
2. What are "holy tempers"? What effect do they have on our hearts and lives?
3. If John Wesley saw the contemporary bumper sticker that reads "Christians aren't perfect, just forgiven" would he agree or disagree? Why?
4. How does one grow in Christian perfection?

---

36. "Christian Perfection," ¶ I.9, *Works* 2:104–5.
37. "On Faith," ¶ II.5, *Works* 3:501.

7

THE MEANS OF GRACE

ON WORKING OUT OUR OWN SALVATION

We have seen that the entire way of salvation, from the inception of conscience to being restored to the image of God, is a work of the Holy Spirit, grounded in what God has done through Jesus Christ. But we have also seen how grace is relational, both enabling and seeking human response, drawing persons into an ongoing relationship.

Reflecting on Philippians 2:12–13 ("work out your own salvation with fear and trembling: for it is God that worketh in you, both to will and to do of his good pleasure"), Wesley developed his most careful and mature discussion of grace and human response in his sermon "On Working Out Our Own Salvation."[1] There he showed the interconnection between God working in us and our working by making two central claims. "First, God worketh in you; therefore you can work—otherwise it would be

1. "On Working Out Our Own Salvation," *Works* 3:199.

impossible."[2] This is how Wesley understood that salvation is by grace alone—that without it, we would be unable to respond to God. "Secondly," he continued, "God worketh in you; therefore you *must* work: you must be 'workers together with him' (they are the very words of the Apostle); otherwise he will cease working."[3] Here we see the intrinsic relationality of salvation, in that for a relationship to grow both sides must be actively participating in it. We cannot grow in the knowledge and love of God unless we are faithfully and receptively engaged with God, and actively serving God in the world.

The way we work out our salvation is through participation in the means of grace. Wesley defined means of grace to be "outward signs, words, or actions ordained of God, and appointed for this end—to be the *ordinary* channels whereby he might convey to men preventing, justifying, or sanctifying grace."[4] In his sermon "The Means of Grace," probably written in the 1740s to deal with the lingering after-effects of the controversy with the Moravian stillness teaching, Wesley recognized that there are many who abuse the means of grace by mistaking "the *means* for the *end*, and to place religion rather in doing those outward works than in a heart renewed after the image of God."[5] But contrary to the Moravians, the antidote to this dead formalism is not to abandon the means of grace but to wait for grace in the means God "hath ordained; in using, not in laying them aside."[6] While not ruling out God acting in an extraordinary manner, Wesley believed we should faithfully

2. Ibid., ¶ III.3, *Works* 3:206.
3. Ibid., ¶ III.7, *Works* 3:208.
4. "The Means of Grace," ¶ II.1, *Works* 1:381.
5. Ibid., ¶ I.2, *Works* 1:378.
6. Ibid., ¶ II.8, *Works* 1:384.

attend to these appointed ordinary means in which God has promised to meet us.

In describing the means of grace Wesley used more than one typology. One classification distinguishes between *instituted* and *prudential* means of grace. The instituted include (1) "Prayer: private, family, public; consisting of deprecation, petition, intercession, thanksgiving"; (2) searching the Scripture by reading (daily, accompanied by prayer and practicing what is learned); (3) the Lord's Supper; (4) fasting; and (5) Christian conference (rightly ordered conversation that ministers grace to hearers).[7] These Wesley believed to be instituted by Christ in the New Testament, and thus of universal import for the church in all ages.

The prudential means include rules "for avoiding evil" and "doing good"; Methodist society, class and band meetings; and "visiting the sick" (indeed, all acts of compassion to others.)[8] Prudential means are practices proven to be helpful for maintaining and growing in our relationship with God, but are subject to change with time and circumstances.

While instituted and prudential means "may be used without fruit"—that is, they can become a dead formalism when persons do not approach them in an open and receptive manner—"there are some means that cannot." These Wesley called *general* means of grace: watching ("against the world, the devil, ourselves"); self-denial; taking up one's cross daily; and exercising the presence of God (endeavoring "to set God always before you.")[9] These are classic spiritual practices that by their very nature cannot be done without being beneficial.

---

7. "'Large Minutes,' 1753–63," *Works* 10:855–57.
8. Ibid., *Works* 10:857.
9. Ibid., *Works* 10:857–58.

Self-denial is so important Wesley devoted a sermon to it, drawing on Jesus' words in Luke 9:23, "If any man will come after me, let him deny himself, and take up his cross daily and follow me."[10] Self-denial is essential to our post-fallen state, where our will is compromised by sin. Thus to "deny ourselves is to deny our own will where it does not fall in with the will of God..."[11] This enables us to "take up our cross" and follow Jesus.

Wesley made an important distinction between "taking up a cross" and "bearing a cross." We are "said to 'bear our cross' when we endure what is laid upon us without our choice, with meekness and resignation." In contrast, "we do not properly 'take up our cross' but when we voluntarily suffer what it is in our power to avoid; when we willingly embrace the will of God, though contrary to our own..."[12]

Failure to utilize these general means of grace is the primary reason people do not continue along the way of salvation, and neglect the other means of grace. Wesley argued that "it is always owing to the want either of self-denial or taking up his cross" that persons do not follow their Lord and become fully disciples of Christ.[13]

A second typology of means of grace became increasingly common in Wesley's writings: *works of piety* and *works of mercy*. Works of piety are those means of grace where the object is God, and primarily consist of those listed under instituted means in the previous typology. While these "ordinances of God" are generally thought to be equivalent to "means of grace," Wesley asked if there are not other means God uses "ordinarily to convey his grace to them that either love or fear him" Surely, he said, there are also works

---

10. "Self-Denial," *Works* 2:238.
11. Ibid., ¶ I.6, *Works* 2:243.
12. Ibid., ¶ I.11, *Works* 2:244.
13. Ibid., ¶ II. 6–7, *Works* 2:274–78.

of mercy.[14] Wesley described works of mercy as using "all diligence in feeding the hungry, clothing the naked, visiting them that are sick or in prison," as well as using all means in one's "power to save souls from death."[15]

We can see why this second typology was so attractive to Wesley if we look at its inner logic in two ways. First, works of piety and works of mercy are how one lives out the Christian life. Awakened sinners do these works as acts of obedience; those growing in sanctification do them as acts of love—holiness of heart produces holiness of life. What Wesley saw is that as we do them with any degree of faith, the Holy Spirit works through them to enable our continued growth. Second, if we are to grow in the knowledge and love of God, and in love for our neighbor, these means of grace are designed for that very end. As I have argued elsewhere, a relationship entails being present in some way to another, as well as coming to know the identity or character of another; in other words, *who* that other is.[16] The works of piety, most especially scripture, the Lord's Supper, and the prayers of the church, provide descriptive access to the identity of God—God's character, what God has done, and what God has promised—as well as a means to encounter God through faith. Works of mercy enable us to know our neighbor, and to encounter God in and through the neighbor.

Wesley could not conceive of growth in salvation apart from participation in the means of grace. But he was well aware of the difficulties that can hinder that participation.

---

14. "On Visiting the Sick," ¶ 1, *Works* 3:385; see also "The Scripture Way of Salvation," ¶ III, 9–10, *Works* 2:166, and "On Working Out Our Own Salvation," ¶ 4, *Works* 3:205–6.

15. "On Zeal," ¶ III.9, *Works* 3:319.

16. See Knight, *The Presence of God in the Christian Life*.

Thus the heart of his organizational structure was designed to encourage persons to faithfully use the means of grace.

DISCIPLINE IN COMMUNITY

By 1743 Wesley had drawn up a set of rules for his societies designed to encourage his Methodists to use the means of grace. Otherwise known as the Methodist "discipline," commitment to these rules was what made one a Methodist. Admission into a Methodist society had one condition: "a desire to flee the wrath to come," to be saved from one's sins (that is, to be an awakened sinner). But, Wesley said, "wherever this is really fixed in the soul it will be shown by its fruits"; therefore those who desire to remain in a society "should continue to evidence their desire of salvation" by adhering to these rules.[17]

Although Wesley listed under the first two rules a number of specifics that were prevalent concerns in his context, it is the three rules themselves that provided the framework within which Methodists sought to live. The first rule was to evidence a desire for salvation "By doing no harm, by avoiding evil in every kind—especially that which is most generally practiced." This is a turning away from actions, practices, values and ways of life that take us away from God and our neighbor, and includes such harmful activities as quarrelling, dishonesty in business, "uncharitable or unprofitable conversation," and "laying up treasures on earth."[18] This rule corresponds to the general means of grace, especially watching and self-denial.

The second rule was to evidence a desire for salvation "By doing good, by being in every kind merciful after their

---

17. "The Nature, Design, and General Rules of the United Societies," ¶ 4, *Works* 9:70.

18. Ibid., *Works* 9:71.

power, as they have opportunity..." to the bodies and souls of others. This corresponds to works of mercy (although Wesley also spoke here of the general means of grace of self-denial and taking up one's cross as foundational to doing good).[19] This second rule reinforces Wesley's oft-repeated observation that being a Christian does not only mean refraining from that which is harmful to oneself or others, but more positively engaging in actions of compassion and care for one's neighbor.

The third rule was to evidence a desire for salvation "By attending upon all the ordinances of God." The specific practices Wesley listed here correspond with works of piety.[20]

This discipline was designed to aid persons in their relationship to God and neighbor through the various means of grace. But it became evident that even the best intentioned had difficulty consistently keeping to it, most especially at the beginning. The central reason for this was "dissipation."

Dissipation was a term that had become prevalent to the point of overuse in Wesley's day. Popularly the term designated a certain pattern of outward behavior, namely persons "who are violently attached to women, gaming, drinking; to dances, balls, races," or fox hunting.[21] But Wesley goes to its root meaning—to disperse or scatter—and applies it more broadly. Our "desires are dissipated," he argued "when they are unhinged from God, their proper centre, and scattered to and fro among the poor, perishing, unsatisfying things of the world."[22] There are "a thousand things which daily occur that are apt to dissipate our

19. Ibid., *Works* 9:72.
20. Ibid., *Works* 9:73.
21. "On Dissipation," ¶ 12, *Works* 3:120.
22. Ibid., ¶ 10, *Works* 3:120.

thoughts, and distract us from attending to" the voice of God "continually speaking to our hearts."[23] This includes not only persons focused on the "hurry of business," "seeking honour or preferment," or "diversions" and "silly pleasures," but also anyone "who forgets God by a close attention to any worldly employment." Thus the person who "is habitually inattentive to the presence and will of his Creator, he is a 'dissipated' man."[24] Dissipation "is the art of forgetting God."[25]

Dissipation, then, is when the many distractions of life, whether deplorable, admirable, or everyday, draw us away from God. As other things become more central in our lives, God is gradually moved to the periphery. When that occurs, although we still believe there is a God, we for all practical purposes become atheists, living our lives as if there were no God.

Faith is the cure for dissipation in that it enables us to know and trust in God. It is what keeps the means of grace from becoming simply an external routine rather than means to encountering God. But at the same time faith is vulnerable to dissipation. Thus we need a way to counter dissipation by nurturing faith.

Initially it seemed that uniting his Methodists together in societies would nurture their growth. At the beginning Wesley noted that those who were awakened but did not come together with others tended to fall away, while most of those who were united together continued to grow.[26] "But as much as we endeavored to watch over each other,"

23. Ibid., ¶ 6, *Works* 3:118.

24. Ibid., ¶ 12, *Works* 3:120.

25. "On Walking by Sight and Walking by Faith," ¶ 20, *Works* 4:58.

26. "A Plain Account of the People Called Methodists," ¶ I.9, *Works* 9:257-8.

Wesley said, "we soon found some who did not 'live the gospel.'" Indeed "several grew cold, and gave way to the sins which had long easily beset them." As the movement grew, so did the numbers in the societies, such that Wesley was no longer able to observe, advise or correct his people. The result was not only detrimental to them but to others. Having such "disorderly walkers" among them brought scandal to the movement as well as temptation and discouragement among the Methodists.[27]

The solution to this problem came by accident. In 1742 at a meeting of the society in Bristol, Wesley led a discussion concerning how they might retire the debt incurred in building their preaching chapel, called the New Room. It was suggested that the society be divided into *classes* of around twelve persons each, and the leader of each class would collect a penny from each member (and pay on behalf of those who were too poor to contribute). As the leaders visited they discovered members who were not living in accordance with the discipline.[28] Wesley quickly made the primary responsibility of the leaders "To see each person in his class once a week at the least; in order to inquire how their souls prosper; To advise, reprove, comfort, or exhort, as occasion may require; [and] To receive what they are willing to give toward the relief of the poor."[29]

Given the difficulties of visiting each member separately, it was soon decided to have the entire class meet weekly. There advice was given, "quarrels made up, misunderstandings removed"; members "began to 'bear one another's burdens', and . . . to 'care for each other.'"[30] It was at

27. Ibid., ¶ II.1–2, *Works* 9:260.

28. Ibid., ¶ II.3, *Works* 9:260–1; see also "Thoughts Upon Methodism," ¶ 5, *Works* 9:528.

29. Ibid., ¶ III.5, *Works* 9:261.

30. Ibid., ¶ 6–7, *Works* 9:262.

these meetings the members had regular accountability for whether or not they were keeping the discipline. The classes were made features of all the societies, and from then on to be a Methodist in Wesley's connection was to commit to the discipline and attend the weekly class meeting.

This, then, was how dissipation was ultimately addressed. Methodists attended a weekly meeting in which they would give an account of how they had done trying to keep to the discipline the week prior. That they would be coming to the meeting was itself a strong incentive to remain focused on the practices prescribed in the rules.

Once they were established Wesley never doubted the essential role of classes for all Methodists, but most especially for awakened sinners. Writing in 1763, he said "I was more convinced than ever that the preaching like an apostle, without joining together those that are awakened and training them up in the ways of God, is only begetting children for the murderer,"[31] that is, for Satan.

Discipline in community was for Wesley the central organizational feature designed to assist his Methodists in Christian growth. While the classes were foundational, there were additional small groups that met weekly and addressed more specific needs along the way of salvation. The most important of these were the *bands*.

The bands predate the classes—they were borrowed by Wesley from the Moravians, and modified to address the specific needs of those growing in sanctification. They differed from classes in both size and composition. Bands were smaller than classes, consisting of 8–10 members. They were also organized by gender and marital status, such that there were bands for married men, married women, unmarried men, and unmarried women. This was done to facilitate freer conversation, as the focus of the bands was

---

31. "Journal," August 25, 1763, *Works* 21:424.

The Means of Grace

on inward sin. There people could "pour out their hearts without reserve, particularly with regard to the sin which did still 'easily beset' them, and the temptations which were most apt to prevail over them."[32] Thus their discussion, unlike the class meeting, was highly confessional in nature, aiding growth in sanctification by dealing forthrightly with the sin remaining in the heart.

Wesley was clear that classes and bands were at the heart of Methodism. "Never omit meeting your class or band," he wrote, "never absent yourself from any public meeting. These are the very sinews of our Society."[33] While a majority of Methodists were not actually in bands, their importance should not be underestimated. If the goal of salvation is to restore persons to the image of God, then the bands were critical to that process. The band meeting was, as Kevin M. Watson has so aptly put it, "the engine of holiness in Methodism."[34]

In addition to classes and bands, two other small groups played significant roles in Wesley's movement. *Penitent bands* were for those who "fell from the faith, either all at once, by falling into known, willful sin, or gradually, and almost insensibly, by giving way in what they called little things—by sins of omission, by yielding to heart sins, or by not watching unto prayer." Their faith weakened, they now wanted to regain what they had lost. By creating a meeting where "all the hymns, exhortations, and prayers are adapted to their circumstances," many not only recovered their faith but grew in it with greater strength than before.[35]

---

32. "A Plain Account of the People Called Methodists," ¶ VI.2, *Works* 9:266.

33. "Farther Thoughts Upon Christian Perfection," Q. 37, *Works* 13:120.

34. Watson, *Pursuing Social Holiness*, 94.

35. "A Plain Account of the People Called Methodists," ¶ VII.1–2, and VIII.1, *Works* 9:268–69.

The other group was the *select society* for those who had grown in sanctification. These were directed to "press after perfection," and incited "to love one another more, and to watch more carefully over each other . . ." Unlike classes and bands, the meeting was unstructured, marked by "free conversation," for "in a multitude of counselors there is safety."[36]

Wesley enforced this community-centered discipline, especially with regard to classes and bands, through issuing quarterly *tickets* to those who sought to keep the discipline and faithfully attended the weekly meetings. Those who did not receive tickets were no longer considered members of the society and could not attend its quarterly meeting. This also meant that they could not attend one of the central features of those meetings, the *love feast*. Borrowed from the Moravians, the love feast consisted of a meal of plain cakes and water within the context of fellowship, prayer, and especially testimony. It was the testimonies that made the love feast so popular, for there persons gave witness to what God was doing in their lives since they last met together. It was a strong means to encourage participants to trust in God with an expectant faith and to grow toward or in sanctification.

THE SACRAMENTS

While there is little question that he considered the two Protestant sacraments to be means of grace, Wesley always called the Lord's Supper a means of grace but never baptism. The most likely reason for this is that the Lord's Supper is repeated and intended for Christian growth, while baptism occurs only once and has as its purpose initiation. Corresponding to this Wesley spoke clearly and deeply about

---

36. Ibid., ¶ VIII 2, 4, *Works* 9:207.

the theology of the Lord's Supper, while his comments on baptism were more ambiguous and have led to a variety of interpretations.

The strong desire of the Wesley brothers to partake of the Lord's Supper as often as possible goes back to their Holy Club days, and that same desire became a central characteristic of the spirituality of Wesley's Methodists. In contrast to the minimalist position of the Latitudinarians that a person need not receive communion more than three times a year, or even the High Church preference for "frequent" communion, Wesley argued "that it is the duty of every Christian to receive the Lord's Supper as often as he can."[37] The grounds of his argument for "constant communion" is twofold: it is "a command of God" and "a mercy to man,"[38] that is, a means of grace.

In light of this, Wesley's Methodists desired weekly communion, which was largely not possible as most Anglican churches offered it less frequently. Methodists would show up in large numbers wherever communion was available, even in houses where it was taken to the sick. Meeting this demand was a continual problem. The Wesley brothers grew flexible about location, providing the Lord's Supper in their preaching chapels and other places outside of church buildings. But they held firm to its being offered only by ordained clergy, a principle that would eventually lead John Wesley to take the extraordinary step of ordaining some of his lay preachers to increase the sacrament's availability.

This hunger for the Lord's Supper was fueled by the expectancy with which it was approached. For the Wesleys, as Lorna Khoo notes, the focus of the Lord's Supper "was not on the faith (nor of the worthiness) of the recipient," but "on the reality of a dynamic encounter with the presence of

37. "The Duty of Constant Communion," I.1, *Works* 3:428.
38. Ibid., II.2, *Works* 3:431.

Christ."³⁹ All were invited to the table, and there all could come into the presence of Jesus Christ.

Here we see a concrete example of the mediated immediacy that John Wesley argued as an alternative to Moravian stillness in the Fetter Lane controversy. But it also shows that what Wesley envisions is not some static reception of "grace" as if it is something apart from God, but a personal and transforming encounter with Jesus Christ. This meal involves not only our minds but our hearts; it powerfully conveys to us God's love for us in Christ.

Christ is present in the Lord's Supper through the power of the Holy Spirit. John Calvin would speak of the Spirit uniting us with Christ such that our thoughts are raised to heaven where Christ is. But with Wesley, as Theodore Runyon observes, "*the direction is reversed.* Rather than our thoughts rising to heaven, *the Spirit brings Christ to us . . .*"⁴⁰ This means that our hearts are being infused with the life of heaven in this life, in sanctification. It also means, as Khoo describes it, that Wesleyan spirituality "placed the Spirit alongside the struggling believer, initiating, inspiring, encouraging, correcting, and leading the person into deeper consecration of heart and life."⁴¹

This powerful theology of the Lord's Supper took deep root among Wesley's Methodists through the wide availability of the *Hymns on the Lord's Supper*, published in 1745. This work contained John Wesley's abridged and edited version of Daniel Brevint's popular work, *The Christian Sacrament and Sacrifice*, plus 166 hymns by Charles Wesley largely arranged according to Brevint's categories. In the hands of the Wesleys, Brevint's spirituality becomes much more experiential and relational.

---

39. Khoo, *Wesleyan Eucharistic Spirituality*, 56.
40. Runyon, *New Creation*, 130.
41. Khoo, *Wesleyan Eucharistic Spirituality*, 196.

The Means of Grace

The major categories in both Brevint and Wesley are sacrament and sacrifice. "Sacrament" refers to God using the Lord's Supper to offer us the blessings of salvation, and "sacrifice" is our offering in return, our grateful response in love and service. This is the fundamentally relational character of this sacrament that marks all the works of piety. As a "sacrament" the Lord's Supper enables us to encounter Christ in three ways: (1) it represents "the sufferings of Christ which are *past*, whereof it is a memorial"; (2) it conveys "the first fruits of these sufferings, in *present graces*, whereof it is a means"; and (3) it assures "us of *glory to come*, whereof it is an infallible pledge."[42] Thus there is a past, present and future dimension to this sacrament, but one in which all three dimensions are experienced as realities in the present.

When we recall that faith is a spiritual sense enabling us to encounter past and future events in our present, we can see how this is so in the Lord's Supper. The sufferings of Christ are in the past, yet in this meal we "see" them, and they have an impact on our lives, evoking remorse at our sins which led to the cross but also joy and gratitude for the inexpressible love that led the Son of God to die for us. The same can be said of the future: Jesus has not returned, yet in this meal we already experience our presence at the eschatological feast. Thus this meal is not simply a matter of recalling things to mind but actually experiencing them anew; it is, in Khoo's words, the event where the "time-transcending Christ, presented against a Trinitarian background, breaks out of theological time-bound categories applied to the eucharist."[43] Is it any wonder, then, that Wesley's Methodists, their expectancy shaped by Charles

---

42. Rattenbury, *Eucharistic Hymns*, 176.
43. Khoo, *Wesleyan Eucharistic Spirituality*, 68.

Wesley's hymns, sought to receive the sacrament whenever and wherever they could?

If Wesley saw the Lord's Supper as a sacrament to be embraced, he found baptism a problem to be addressed. The fundamental issue was that most in England had been baptized as infants, but most did not seem to be living the religion of the heart. There was a disconnect between the act of baptism and the actuality of the new birth in human hearts and lives.

Wesley thus homed in on those who say they do not need a new birth because they are baptized. In 1748 Wesley exhorted "Lean no more on the staff of that broken reed, that ye *were* born again in baptism. Who denies ye were then made 'children of God and heirs of the Kingdom of heaven'? But not withstanding this, ye are now children of the devil; therefore ye must be born again."[44] In a 1760 sermon Wesley further developed his argument by stating that "baptism is not the new birth; they are not one and the same thing."[45] In a sacrament there is a distinction between the sign (in this case, water) and the thing signified (death unto sin and new birth by the Spirit); to have the outward sign is of no avail without the inward grace.

This is sometimes called Wesley's "evangelical" understanding of baptism. But it is in tension with his more "sacramental" understanding. This is seen in his repeated affirmation of the baptismal regeneration of infants. In that same 1760 sermon he said that "our Church supposes that all who are baptized in their infancy are at the same time born again.[46] In the case of adults, however, new birth may or may not occur at the time of their baptism.

---

44. "The Marks of the New Birth," ¶ IV.5, *Works* 1:430.
45. "The New Birth," ¶ IV.1, *Works* 2:196.
46. Ibid., ¶ IV.2, *Works* 2:197.

The Means of Grace

The sacramental side of Wesley's theology is most fully stated in his 1758 *A Treatise on Baptism*. There he described baptism as a sacrament of initiation that enters us into a covenant with God and into the church. We are adopted as children of God in that "By *water* . . . as a means . . . we are regenerated or born again." But this grace is not irresistible, hence we can lose that grace if "we quench the Holy Spirit of God by long-continued wickedness."[47]

How might this tension in Wesley's theology of baptism be explained? One influential interpretation is that of Bernard Holland, who argues that Wesley believed in *two* regenerations: one for children through baptism, the second for adults through conversion.[48] This would place Wesley in agreement with many Pietists. In contrast, Ole Borgen insists Wesley accepted his own Anglican tradition's teaching on baptismal regeneration, and thus believed one could receive regeneration as an infant and continue in it throughout adulthood. But should one fall away from it, as most did, one then needed to be born anew.[49] More recently Ted Campbell, noting that Wesley did not believe regeneration invariably accompanied adult baptisms, argues this puts him more at odds with Catholic, Orthodox, and Lutheran theologies of baptism, but more in line with the Reformed tradition, which has held regeneration may occur before, during or after baptism, or even without baptism at all.[50] Campbell's interpretation is further supported by Wesley's belief that baptism, while commanded by Christ, was not absolutely necessary for salvation, for "If it were every Quaker must be damned, which I can in no wise believe."[51]

---

47. "A Treatise on Baptism," ¶ II.4, *Works* (J) 10:191–92.
48. Holland, *Baptism in Early Methodism*.
49. Borgen, *John Wesley on the Sacraments*.
50. Campbell, "Conversion and Baptism in Wesleyan Spirituality."
51. "Letter to the Revd. Gilbert Boyce," May 22, 1750, *Works*

What can be said with certainly is that Wesley viewed baptism, like all means of grace, as relational. "*Baptism doth now save us,*" he writes in the Treatise, "if we live answerable thereto—if we repent, believe, and obey the gospel..."[52] Our response to baptismal grace, then, is lifelong. But if we are unfaithful Wesley insisted God remains faithful, and reaches out in love to restore us once again to new life in Christ.

DISCUSSION QUESTIONS

1. In what way do we "work out our own salvation"?
2. What are "means of grace? And why are they important?
3. What did Wesley mean by "self-denial"?
4. What was the original Methodist "discipline"?
5. What is "dissipation" and why is it a danger to the Christian life?
6. How did classes and bands aid early Methodists in growing as Christians?
7. Why was the Lord's Supper so important to early Methodists?

26:425.

52. "A Treatise on Baptism," ¶ II.5, *Works* (J) 10:192.

8

RELIEVING THE DISTRESS OF THE NEIGHBOR

GOOD NEWS TO THE POOR

LOVE, IF IT IS truly the love that was made manifest in Jesus Christ, must be lived out in service to others. While it is love for God that is the reigning disposition in the hearts of newborn Christians, it is that very love for God that requires a certain priority be given to works of mercy over works of piety. "Whenever . . . one interferes with the other," Wesley said, "works of mercy are to be preferred." God seeks mercy over sacrifice, hence works of piety are to be omitted or postponed "when we are called to relieve the distress of our neighbor, whether in body or soul."[1] The primary way this took place among Wesley's Methodists was through ministry to the poor.

---

1. "On Zeal," ¶ II.9, *Works* 3:314.

The roots of this concern for the poor lie in the Holy Club. From then on it became a focus of John and Charles Wesley and a defining feature of their Methodism. John Wesley led by example. "I bear the rich, and love the poor," he wrote in 1764; "Therefore I spend *almost all* my time with them."[2] The same can be said of other leaders in the movement. Wesley's chief ally John Fletcher turned down more lucrative parishes to take the church in Madely, primarily because he felt called by God to minister to those engaged in the new and dangerous occupations of mining and iron making.[3]

The poor in Wesley's England were largely the working poor, living on subsistence wages and often lacking job security. They were poor because they "lacked the necessities of life," such as food, clothing, and adequate places to live; as a consequence they were especially subject to disease and other misfortunes.[4] Describing the conditions of workers in Manchester's burgeoning cotton industry, Steve Rankin speaks of many as "living in the basement 'apartments'" below street level, "with raw sewage running in the ditches outside a solitary window opening with no way to close it." These "tenements were hopelessly infested with vermin and all kinds of diseases."[5]

Funded by collections for the poor at society and class meetings, Wesley responded with a diversity of ministries. These included, as Douglas Meek notes, "feeding, clothing, housing the poor; preparing the unemployed for work and finding them employment; visiting the poor, sick and prisoners; devising new forms of health care education and delivery for the indigent; distributing books to the needy;

---

2. "Letter to Ann Foard," September 29, 1764, *Works* 27:391.
3. Trinder, "John Fletcher's Parishioners," 29.
4. Heitzenrater, *Poor and the People Called Methodists*, 27–28.
5. Rankin, "People Called Methodists," 41.

and raising structural questions about an economy that produced poverty."[6] Wesley not only sought financial support for these ministries, but urged his Methodists to visit the poor and build relationships with them.

One reason for visiting the poor was to shatter pervasive stereotypes. Commenting on his own visiting the poor in 1753, Wesley wrote that "I found some in their cells underground, others in their garrets, half starved both with cold and hunger, added to weakness and pain. But I found not one of them unemployed who was able to crawl about the room." Wesley concluded, "So wickedly devilishly false is that common objection, 'They are poor only because they are idle.'"[7] Failure to become acquainted with the lives of the poor can have devastating effects on one's own Christian growth. "One great reason why the rich in general have so little sympathy for the poor," Wesley observed, "is because they so seldom visit them. Hence it is that . . . one part of the world does not know what the other suffers. Many of them do not know, because they do not care to know: they keep out of the way of knowing it—and then plead their voluntary ignorance as an excuse for their hardness of heart."[8]

Many of Wesley's Methodists not only visited the poor, but organized to do so. Beginning in 1785, Strangers' Friends Societies were formed in London and other large cities where mining and manufacturing drew thousands of displaced workers seeking employment. Through these ministries Methodists lived out their love for others by seeking to meet a wide range of material needs such as food, medicine, and even furniture, as well as sharing the good news of Jesus Christ.[9]

6. Meeks, "Introduction," in *Portion of the Poor*, 9–10.
7. "Journal," February 8, 1753, *Works* 20:445.
8. "On Visiting the Sick," ¶ I.3, *Works* 3:387–88.
9. See Macquiban, "Friends of All?"; and Rankin, "The People Called Methodists."

In his 1773 *Thoughts on the Present Scarcity of Provisions* Wesley sought to address some of the systemic causes of widespread hunger in England. The cost of food was now so high, he argued, "that the generality of people are hardly able to buy anything else." Thus they do not have money left to purchase other goods. Unable to sell their products because of this decreased demand, employers could not pay their workers, creating a growing number of unemployed poor who could not afford food at all.[10]

The rise in the cost of food Wesley partly attributes to the increased demand for grain such as wheat, corn, and oats by distilleries and the highly lucrative trade in horses, both for export to France and the carriages of the wealthy. Another significant factor was the enclosure of lands, leading to the eviction of small farmers who sent bacon, pork, poultry and eggs to market, and their replacement by "gentlemen-farmers" who now send none.[11] Even worse was the luxury and waste in the households of aristocrats and the wealthy, who sustain their extravagant life-styles by continually increasing the rents on their lands, forcing many small farmers into near poverty.[12] To all of these could be added the "enormous taxes" collected by the government to service the national debt.[13]

In response to this crisis Wesley called upon the government to enact a number of remedies: prohibition of distilleries, placing a tax on carriages and exports to reduce the number of horses, limiting the size of farms, curtailing luxury, and cutting the national debt in half.[14] Thus while

---

10. "Thoughts on the Present Scarcity of Provisions," ¶ I. 1–2, *Works* (J) 11:52–54.
11. Ibid., ¶ I. 3–6, *Works* (J) 11:54–56.
12. Ibid., ¶ I. 6–7, *Works* (J) 11:56–57.
13. Ibid., ¶ I. 9, *Works* (J) 11:57.
14. Ibid., ¶ II. 1–8, *Works* (J) 11:57–59.

his emphasis was on ministries that alleviated hunger, Wesley was not at all reluctant to call upon government to take action to correct the social and economic conditions that produced widespread hunger.

FREEDOM FOR SLAVES

The strong and unyielding opposition of John and Charles Wesley to slavery began during their time in the Georgia colonies. Although not yet legal in Georgia, they saw slavery first hand in neighboring South Carolina. They were appalled at the barbarity of many slave owners and repulsed by the indignity of the institution itself. Slavery was not only inhumane to the slaves but morally degrading to slave owners and the entire society.

When the antislavery movement in England began its long struggle to end the slave trade as a prelude to abolition itself, John Wesley sought to lend his support. In 1770 Wesley told Granville Sharp that he wanted to produce a tract on the subject. Sharp, an Anglican who had been working through the legal system to fight slavery, provided Wesley with a number of antislavery writings, including those of Anthony Benezet, a Quaker. Their subsequent three-way correspondence led to the publication in 1774 of Wesley's *Thoughts Upon Slavery*.

Unlike most of Wesley's writings, the tract was aimed at a wide audience, and grounded its case in natural law rather than scripture. Nevertheless, as Irv Brendlinger has shown, there was an implicit theological assumption underlying Wesley's argument. His belief in prevenient grace meant Wesley could appeal to the consciences of his readers, believing them to have a basic capacity to distinguish right from wrong and empathize with the suffering of others.[15]

15. Brendlinger, *Social Justice*, 88.

Drawing from Benezet, Wesley laid out a powerful argument. In a previous work I summarized it this way:

> After a brief overview of contemporary African civilization, Wesley relates the degrading and brutal process of procuring, transporting, selling, and utilizing slaves, including their deaths due to inhumane conditions on slave ships and the torture they face at the hands of owners. Wesley then challenges arguments in favor of slavery based on natural order and economic necessity and concludes with a pointed exhortation to slave traders and slave owners appealing to their humanity while warning them of a just God who will judge everyone according to their works.[16]

To those who argued that slavery was "authorized by law," Wesley denied "slave-holding to be consistent with any degree of natural justice." Can law "turn darkness into light, or evil into good," he asked? "Where is the justice of inflicting the severest evils on those who have done us no wrong? . . . of tearing them from their native country, and depriving them of liberty itself, to which an Angolan has the same natural right as an Englishman . . .?" Where is the justice in murdering thousands "in their own land" and "on shipboard" in order to place "tens of thousands in that cruel slavery to which they are so unjustly reduced?"[17]

Notable in Wesley's argument is his belief in human equality. While not all who opposed slavery were egalitarian with regard to race, Wesley insisted "the African is in no respect inferior to the European."[18] Human equality was implicit in Wesley's belief that all persons are created in the

---

16. Knight, *Anticipating Heaven Below*, 212.
17. "Thoughts Upon Slavery," ¶ IV. 2–3., *Works* (J) 11:70.
18. Ibid., ¶ IV. 8, *Works* (J) 11:74.

image of God, all are equally loved by God, and Christ died for all. But in his essay he again appealed to natural law. "Liberty," he said, "is the right of every human creature, as soon as he breaths the vital air; and no human law can deprive him of that right which he derives from the law of nature." Thus if "you have any regard to justice (to say nothing of mercy, nor the revealed law of God) render unto all their due."[19]

Thoughts Upon Slavery was both inexpensive and widely circulated, and had an immediate impact, drawing Methodists and non-Methodists alike into the fight against slavery. However, Wesley's appeals to the consciences of slave traders and slave owners fell largely on deaf ears. By 1787 Wesley was advocating for Parliamentary action to outlaw the slave trade and urging readers of his *Arminian Magazine* to sign petitions supporting that effort.[20] The last letter Wesley wrote in his life was to William Wilberforce, encouraging him to persevere in his efforts in Parliament to bring an end to slavery.

HEALING THE BODY

While disease and other afflictions were widespread in eighteenth century England, hope of being delivered from them was not. Partly this was due to both the lack of availability and often ineffectiveness of medical care. But there were religious reasons as well. Since the Reformation the dominant Protestant view was that miracles of healing ended with the apostolic age and could not be expected in the present. Instead the common assumption of Wesley's contemporaries was that illness was sent by God, and the proper response to it was with faith, perhaps accompanied

---

19. Ibid., ¶ V. 6, *Works* (J) 11:79.
20. Brendlinger, *Social Justice*, 143.

by repentance. While most did not see this as a barrier to receiving medical care, it strongly encouraged a spirituality of resignation rather than hope.

Charles Wesley generally manifested this spirituality of resignation, but John Wesley did not. It simply was not congruent with John Wesley's understanding of God's love, power and purposes. It also was at odds with his diagnosis of the problem. While not ruling out God sending or using affliction for particular spiritual purposes, the basic cause for human affliction is living in a fallen world.

John Wesley argued that the source of human maladies is the disharmony introduced onto the created order by our fall into sin. While in the beginning the entire creation was harmonious and interrelated, with each "part exactly suited to the others,"[21] the fall disrupted that harmony, though not the interrelation of the parts. Now the various parts of creation are inescapably in conflict with one another. Humanity turned from God and became mortal; as a consequence "seeds of weakness and pain, of sickness and death, are now lodged in our inmost substance; whence a thousand disorders continually spring, even without the aid of external violence."[22]

This creational disharmony also had a detrimental effect on the relation of human bodies and souls. Because the body was now corruptible it "very frequently hinders the soul in its operations, and at best serves it imperfectly. Yet the soul cannot dispense with its service, imperfect as it is. For an embodied spirit cannot form one thought but by the mediation of its bodily organs." Thus "every disorder of the body, especially of the parts more immediately subservient to thinking, lays an almost insuperable bar in the way of its

---

21. "God's Approbation of His Works," ¶ I. 14, *Works* 2:396.
22. Preface to *Primitive Physick*, ¶ 2, *Works* (J) 14:308.

thinking justly."[23] This is why we never fully escape in this life those mistaken ideas and misjudgments that produce involuntary transgressions.

In the new creation to come God will restore and even enhance the original harmony, and sin, sickness and death will be no more. But as we have just seen, Wesley's optimism of grace led him to expect greater harmony in this present age as well.

The reverse is also the case: a distressed soul can produce bodily effects. "The passions," Wesley noted, "have a greater influence on health than most people are aware of." The "violent and sudden passions" can produce "acute diseases," while "slow and lasting passions, such as grief and hopeless love, bring on chronical diseases." Until "the passion which caused the disease is calmed, medicine is applied in vain." It is the "love of God," said Wesley, that "is the sovereign remedy of all miseries"; it prevents bodily disorders "by keeping the passions themselves within due bounds." Through "the unspeakable joy, and perfect calm, serenity, and tranquility it gives the mind, it becomes the most powerful of all the means of health and long life."[24] Indeed he saw how God was already at work restoring persons to health, through medicine, healthy living, and prayer.

Wesley's concern for health and healing grew out of his ministry, especially with those in the lower classes. He was "in pain for many of the poor that were sick; there was so great expense, and so little profit." Finding neither hospitals nor physicians to be of much help, Wesley "thought of a kind of desperate expedient, 'I will prepare and give them physic myself.'" He had been studying "anatomy and physic" for well over two decades. So enlisting "an apothecary and an experienced surgeon," in 1747 Wesley opened

23. "On the Fall of Man," ¶ II.2, *Works* 2:405–6.
24. Preface to *Primitive Physick*, ¶ VI. 1–5, *Works* (J) 14:316.

dispensaries in London and Bristol. He invited "all who were ill of *chronical* distempers (for I did not care to venture upon *acute*)" to come "and I would give them the best advice I could, and the best medicine I had."[25]

That Wesley would provide medical advice to the poor was not in itself unusual. Giving medical advice (or "physick") to poor parishioners was considered an aspect of the responsibilities of any conscientious Anglican priest, especially if in the High Church tradition. As Deborah Madden has argued, "Wesley felt a *duty* and obligation to practice physick."[26] However Wesley did not have a parish but a renewal movement; thus his ministry was directed to the entirety of Great Britain. What was radical about Wesley's approach was the extent of the people he sought to help and the lengths he was prepared to go to provide that help.

Wesley's greatest impact was not through his dispensaries, which were discontinued after a number of years, but his publication in 1747 of *Primitive Physick: An Easy and Natural Way of Curing Most Diseases*. Going through many editions and widely read on both sides of the Atlantic well into the nineteenth century, this was, in Deborah Madden's words "a manual designed to help the laboring poor stave off disease by regulating their lifestyle through regimen, as well as self-medicating safely when they became sick."[27]

Primitive Physick contained remedies for around 250 maladies. The word "primitive" in the title referred not to the remedies but to the primitive church, which honored physicians who served the poor without recompense. This was in conscious contrast to some eighteenth century physicians who used their expertise to enrich themselves,

---

25. "A Plain Account of the People Called Methodists," ¶ XII. 1–3, *Works* 9:275–76.

26. Madden, *"Cheap, Safe, and Natural Medicine,"* 47.

27. Madden, "Saving Souls and Saving Lives," 6.

and were only interested in patients with the means to pay. But while the approach was primitive the remedies themselves were modern. While many seem strange to us today, Madden reminds us that they were drawn by Wesley from "authoritative medical sources,"[28] and represented what was then the best medical knowledge.

Wesley sought to provide remedies that were "experimental," congruent with the long tradition of medicine beginning in the ancient world which "was wholly founded on experiment," thus attending to those remedies that proved to be effective. Wesley was concerned that eighteenth century medicine, in its desire to be modern, increasingly was becoming theory based, setting "experience aside, to build physic upon hypothesis, to form theories of diseases and their cure and to substitute these in place of experiments."[29] Not only did some physicians tenaciously hold to their theory-driven treatments even when ineffective, but the highly technical nature of this approach gave physicians an expertise that put physick "quite out of the reach of ordinary men."[30]

Wesley intended *Primitive Physick* to put basic healthcare back into the hands of ordinary people. As Madden notes, "the remedies contained within *Primitive Physick* are empirically based from beginning to end."[31] Moreover, by 1760 Wesley began to emphasize those remedies with the best track record by noting them with the word "tried."[32] Just as Wesley valued both testimony and changed lives as "experimental" evidence of the reliability of the promises of

---

28. Madden, *"Cheap, Safe, and Natural Medicine,"* 111.
29. Preface to *Primitive Physick*, ¶ 7, *Works* (J) 14:310.
30. Ibid., ¶ 9, *Works* (J) 14:310.
31. Madden, *"Cheap, Safe, and Natural Medicine,"* 111,
32. Postscript to *Primitive Physick* (1760), *Works* (J) 14:317.

God in salvation, he used evidence of restored health as his criterion for the effectiveness of medical remedies.

In addition to their effectiveness, Wesley sought remedies that were "cheap, safe, and easy medicines; easy to be known, easy to be procured, and easy to be applied by plain, unlettered men." He deliberately omits ("except in a very few cases") "the four Herculean medicines, opium, the bark, steel, and most preparations of quicksilver," all of which are "extremely dangerous" even in the hands of physicians. Instead he recommended "such remedies as air, water, milk, whey, honey, treacle, salt, vinegar, and common English herbs, with a few foreign medicines, almost equally cheap, safe, and common."[33]

Continually revising the *Primitive Physick*, Wesley was attentive to both objections to his remedies and new medical discoveries. Like many others in his day he was convinced of the curative power of low doses of electricity, which he believed "comes the nearest" to being "an universal medicine, of any yet known in the world."[34] To dispense that medicine Wesley owned a small electrifying machine. He was also the first person to make available in popular print the technique of mouth-to-mouth resuscitation.

The *Primitive Physick* also recommended healthy living, both as a general remedy as well as a way for persons "to retain the health they have recovered"[35] Wesley urged his readers to observe "the greatest exactness in your regimen or manner of living. Abstain from all mixed, all high-seasoned, food. Use plain diet, easy of digestion. . . . Drink only water, if it agrees with your stomach; if not, good, clear small beer. Use as much exercise daily, in the open air, as

---

33. Postscript to *Primitive Physick* (1755), ¶ 2–4, *Works* (J) 14:316–7.

34. Postscript to *Primitive Physick* (1780), *Works* (J) 14:318.

35. Preface to *Primitive Physick*, ¶ 16, *Works* (J) 14:314.

you can without weariness." He then elaborated on both food and exercise in great detail, and much of the advice he gave them is still given today.

But as much as Wesley was an advocate of the benefits of medicine and a proper regimen, he was equally a vigorous proponent of "that old unfashionable medicine, prayer." Not only could prayer bring peace to the afflicted, it could be an avenue of divine healing. On one occasion, with regard to his own ailment, Wesley consulted a team of three physicians. "They satisfied me what my disorder was," he said, "and told me there was but one method of cure. Perhaps but one natural one, but I think God has more than one method of healing either the soul or the body."[36]

Wesley believed all healing was from God, and it could occur both through medicine and through prayer. Throughout his long ministry Wesley reported many occasions of miraculous healing that were the result of prayer, be it the prayer of the person afflicted or the prayers of those praying for the person. There is no consistent pattern to these accounts, and unlike some healing theologies today, Wesley did not prescribe formulas or see healing as automatic if one met preconditions. He simply believed in the power of God to heal, recommended prayer for healing, and reported cases in which miraculous healing occured. Nor did he automatically believe every purported instance of healing. As with the Christian life, Wesley assessed each claim on the evidence that a change had occurred.

The day will come when sickness and death will be no more. Wesley believed the same God who is the architect of that new creation was at work even now, restoring health to bodies as well as souls, as an anticipation of that which is to come.

---

36. "Journal," May 18, 1772, *Works* 22:223–24.

DISCUSSION QUESTIONS

1. What are some of the ways Wesley and his Methodists addressed the plight of the poor?
2. What were some of Wesley's arguments against slavery?
3. What were some of the ways Wesley responded to sickness and promoted health?

9

THE LATER CONTROVERSIES

CLAIMING ABSOLUTE PERFECTION

THE LAST THREE DECADES of Wesley's life were marked by controversies, some internal in origin and others external. Whether the issue was the nature of Christian perfection, the antinomian implications of Calvinism, or the nature of the church, what they all had in common was their challenging Wesley's emphasis on holiness of heart and life.

Dominating much of the 1760s was a conflict over the most central and distinctive element in Wesley's theology, Christian perfection. The year 1760 was an encouraging one for proponents of the doctrine. Wesley was encountering instances where increasing numbers of persons were giving credible testimonies to attaining Christian perfection. On March 12, for example, Wesley was in Leeds meeting with people from the surrounding area "who believed they were saved from sin," and spent most of the "day in examining them one by one." While he found he could not give credence to the "testimony of some," with regard to "the far greatest part" it was "plain (unless they could be supposed to tell willful and deliberate lies): (1) that they *feel* no inward sin and to the best of their knowledge, *commit* no outward sin; (2) that they *see* and *love* God every moment . . ., (3) that they have constantly as clear a *witness* from God of sanctification as they have of justification."[1] They were testifying to having received a Christian perfection the same as Wesley had described it. At a Love Feast in London in November Wesley described the "unspeakable change" to which many testified in this way: "After being deeply convinced of inbred sin particularly of pride, anger, self-will, and unbelief, in a moment they *feel* all faith and love: no pride, no self-will, or anger. And from that moment they have continual fellowship with God, always rejoicing, praying, and giving thanks."[2] These are but two of many instances Wesley records during this time.

Wesley believed he was witnessing a remarkable movement of the Holy Spirit bringing persons to experience instantaneous Christian perfection much as they had justification and new birth. He concluded his *Journal* ending in October, 1762, with this observation:

> Many years ago my brother frequently said, "Your day of Pentecost is not fully come. But I doubt not it will, and you will then hear of persons sanctified as frequently as you do now of persons justified." Any unprejudiced reader may observe that it was now fully come. And accordingly, we did hear of persons sanctified in London and most other parts of England, and

1. "Journal," March 12, 1760, *Works* 21:247.
2. Ibid., November 28, 1760 *Works* 21:344.

The Later Controversies

> in Dublin and many other parts of Ireland, as frequently as of persons justified, although instances of the latter were far more frequent than they had been for twenty years before.[3]

In spite of this positive assessment, Wesley was already having to address misunderstandings of Christian perfection. The very prevalence of these experiences seemed to fuel the extravagant claims of some.

At the center of the controversy was Thomas Maxfield, Wesley's first regular lay preacher. Returning to London in August of 1762 after a five months absence, Wesley found, due to Maxfield's influence, persons there "who had more heat than light." Along with his brother, Charles, John had "a long conversation with Mr. Maxfield and freely told him whatever we disliked."[4] At the time they believed the misunderstandings had been successfully addressed, but Maxfield would instead continue to promote his absolutist version of Christian perfection.

The other key figure in the Maxfield camp was lay preacher George Bell. Reluctantly, Wesley came to the conclusion that Bell must not be permitted to preach under Wesley's auspices. Giving him one more chance on December 26, 1762, Wesley found his preaching had become "worse and worse. He now spoke as from God, what I knew God had not spoken." Thus, Wesley concluded, "I therefore desired that he would come thither no more."[5] In February he met with Bell with some others "to convince him of his mistakes, particularly that which he had lately adopted, 'that the end of the world was to be on February the 28th' ... But he was as unmoved as a rock."[6]

---

3. Ibid., October 28, 1762, *Works* 21:392.
4. Ibid., August 17–21, 1762, *Works* 21:386.
5. Ibid., December 26, 1762, *Works* 21:401.
6. Ibid., February 7, 1763, *Works* 21:402.

Wesley's affection for Maxfield and Bell made these encounters painful, even though they were necessary. Some believed he should have much more quickly removed them from his connection. When a woman noted that if she had a servant who failed to follow her directions, she would "discard him at once." Why, then, did Wesley not do the same to Mr. Bell? Wesley responded, "It is right to discard such a *servant*. But what would you do if he were your *son?*"[7]

Tensions within the societies had been building throughout 1761 and by late 1762 had reached a point of crisis. In October 1762, Wesley returned to London to find "the society in an uproar,"[8] with a clear faction siding with Maxfield against Wesley; by February and March of 1763 the schism was complete. Maxfield's followers were gone, declaring John Wesley was now an opponent of Christian perfection.

In October 1762, Wesley wrote a long letter to Maxfield delineating points of agreement and disagreement with regard to doctrine, spirit, and outward behavior. Examining some of the issues Wesley raised with regard to the first two topics will show why this conflict was so dangerous to his movement.

With regard to doctrine, Wesley said, "I like your doctrine of *perfection*, or pure love—love excluding sin," and "insisting that it is merely by *faith*; that consequently it is *instantaneous* . . ." However, Wesley disliked "your supposing man may be as perfect 'as an angel'; that he can be *absolutely* perfect; that he can be *infallible*, or above being *tempted*; or that the moment he is pure in heart he *cannot fall* from it."[9] Maxfield and his allies were teaching a version of Christian perfection similar to that Wesley initially held

7. Ibid., January 1, 1763, *Works* 21:401.
8. Ibid., April 28, 1763, *Works* 21:410.
9. Ibid., October 29, 1762, *Works* 21:394.

but had come to reject. The errors here are multiple, and the threat to the Christian life dire. With this teaching persons could claim, on the basis of having had an intense experience, immunity from both error and temptation.

This leads naturally into Wesley's comments about spirit. While Wesley liked Maxfield's "confidence in God" and "zeal for the salvation of souls," he disliked Maxfield's having "the appearance of *pride*, of overvaluing yourselves and undervaluing others . . ." Indeed Maxfield and his friends speak "of *yourselves* as though *you* were the *only men* who knew and taught the gospel; and as if not *all the clergy* but *all the Methodists* besides, were in utter darkness."[10] There is clear evidence that Maxfield's followers were no longer willing to be taught by others who had not had the same experience as they had. Maxfield himself had written Wesley in October saying "I long to have *your* heart set at full liberty. I know you will *then see things* in a wonderful different light from what it is *possible* to *see them before*."[11]

This pride may have been linked with another of Wesley's concerns: "I dislike something that has the appearance of *enthusiasm*: overvaluing *feelings* and *inward impressions*; mistaking the mere work of *imagination* for the voice of the Spirit; expecting the end without the means; and undervaluing *reason, knowledge*, and *wisdom*, in general."[12] Here is the same sort of concern that led Wesley to oppose Moravian teaching in the Fettter Lane Society, that is, emphasizing immediate experience in opposition to means of grace, and the supposed direct voice of God against reason. Wesley continued to see this as the doorway to self-deception.

There was another dualism Wesley disliked "that has the appearance of *antinomianism*," in which the law is

10. Ibid., *Works* 21:395.
11. Ibid., February 5, 1763, *Works* 21:405.
12. Ibid., October 29, 1763, *Works* 21:396.

dishonored and faith is seen "as contradistinguished from *holiness* than as productive of it."[13] Of course this went right to the core of Wesley's theology, severing the connection between faith and holiness he had so carefully argued for against the Calvinists.

The "appearance" of pride, enthusiasm, and antinomianism raised serious questions concerning whether the perfection claimed by Maxfield was actually Christian perfection at all. But Wesley's final critique of the spirit of Maxfield and his followers removed all doubt:

> But what I most of all dislike is your *littleness of love* to your brethren, to our own society . . . your 'impatience of contradiction'; your counting every man your enemy that reproves or admonishes you in love; your *bigotry* and *narrowness* of spirit, loving in a manner only those that love *you*; your censoriousness, . . . your *divisive spirit*.[14]

"Littleness of love" is not a description of Christian Perfection, nor of sanctification more generally. This, more than anything, undermined their claims. Maxfield and his allies may have had an intense experience, but the fruit they were bearing was not that of Christian perfection. Rather their behavior was actually undermining the credibility of Wesley's teaching.

One person for whom that teaching was undermined was Charles Wesley. Even before 1760 there were subtle but real differences between the two brothers on Christian perfection. As early as 1749 Charles was describing Christian perfection as sinless in an unnuanced way, emphasizing its gradual attainment, and insisting on suffering in both body

13. Ibid.
14. Ibid.

and soul as its prerequisite.[15] When the 1760s controversy broke out, Charles was already inclined to react in ways that put him at odds with his brother. The questions that emerged, as summarized by John Tyson, were these: "(1) Was Charles setting the doctrine of perfection too 'high'? (2) Was Christian perfection an instantaneous blessing or was it received gradually over the course of an entire life? And (3) did perfection occur in the hour of death, or before?"[16] In his *Short Hymns on Select Passages of Scripture* (1762) Charles strongly insisted on gradual perfection, attained at the time of death, and on an ideal if not absolutist definition of perfection. By emphasizing sinlessness in such an unqualified manner, John feared Charles was setting it too high. "*That perfection* which I believe, I can boldly preach, because I think I see five hundred witnesses of it," John wrote, "of *that perfection* which you preach, you do not even think you see any witnesses at all.... Therefore I still think to set perfection *so high* is effectually to renounce it."[17]

Charles Wesley certainly wanted to effectually renounce the claims of Maxfield and Bell. He denied perfection is "caught" in an instant; that one can simply "Believe, and ye are perfect *now*," or that instead of going on to perfection "step by step" we can "Leap o'er the cross to snatch the prize."[18] By insisting on the necessity of suffering and a more absolute perfection he discredited the Maxfield enthusiasts. But in the process he also undercut the careful synthesis John Wesley had constructed between

15. On this see Tyson, *Charles Wesley on Sanctification*, chapter 7.

16. Tyson, *Assist Me to Proclaim*, 246.

17. Cited in ibid., 247.

18. Charles Wesley, "Short Hymn on Heb. 6:1," cited in Tyson, *Charles Wesley: A Reader*, 390.

instantaneous and gradual, intentional sin and involuntary transgressions, and the hope of attaining it through grace prior to the time of death while not making presumptive claims on the basis of experience alone.

THE FEAR OF ANTINOMIANISM

Wesley's life-long commitment to holiness of heart and life as the aim of salvation necessarily required forceful opposition to antinomianism. The antinomian claim that the imputed righteousness of Christ means we need none ourselves, along with the accompanying assumption that salvation only refers to the life to come, was a constant threat to Wesleyans and more moderate Calvinists alike.

With antinomian teachings continuing to lure the unwary Methodist, Wesley decided to address the issue once again at the 1770 annual conference in London. There Wesley posed a question he had originally asked at the 1744 annual conference: Where have his Methodists "leaned too much toward Calvinism?" The answer insisted on the necessity of works as a precondition for justification in two senses. With regard to *final* justification the Minutes argued that holiness is essential, that "every believer, till he comes to glory, work *for* as well as *from* life." With regard to justification as *present* forgiveness the Minutes insisted that "Whoever repents should do 'works meet for repentance.' And if this is not in *order* to find favour, what does he do them for?"[19]

The Minutes further stated that whoever "is *now* accepted of God . . . believes in Christ with a loving obedient heart," but "among those that never heard of Christ" the one accepted "feareth God and worketh righteousness,

---

19. "Annual Minutes of Some Late Conversations, 1770," *Works* 10:392–93.

according to the light he has." This was simply a restatement of Wesley's distinction between the faith of a child of God and the faith of a servant. The *Minutes* insisted this was not "salvation by works"; it was not that "the *merit* of works" is salvific but "works as a *condition*." It concluded by saying that "we are every hour and every moment pleasing or displeasing to God, *according to our works*—according to the whole of our inward tempers, and our outward behaviour."[20]

Even sympathetic accounts of these *Minutes* believe they were loosely worded and ripe for misunderstanding. Just five years earlier, in his sermon "The Scripture Way of Salvation," Wesley was much more precise in his language relating the role of faith and works in justification. There he argued that "both repentance and fruits meet for repentance are in some sense necessary to justification"; but "not in the *same sense* as faith." They "are only *remotely* necessary, necessary in order to faith; whereas faith is *immediately* and *directly* necessary to justification."[21] Thus we are justified by faith alone, but genuine faith is given to those who have repentant hearts and lives. Perhaps if the *Minutes* had been written with this nuance, they would have been less controversial. But they were not, and with their publication a theological firestorm ensued.[22]

At the center of the initial controversy was Selena, the Countess of Huntingdon, and her cousin, the Rev. Walter Shirley, both ardent Calvinists. Lady Huntingdon once had been of a more moderate persuasion when under the influence of George Whitefield and Howell Harris. But

20. Ibid., *Works* 10:393–94.

21. "The Scripture Way of Salvation," ¶ III. 2, *Works* 2:162–63.

22. For a detailed account and analysis of the controversy, see McGonigle, *Sufficient Saving Grace*, chapter 11. See also Collins, *John Wesley*, 216–29.

Whitefield died in America a month after the 1770 conference, and with the influence of Harris waning, the Countess was increasingly allied with those for whom predestination was essential to the gospel.[23]

It did not help that John Wesley preached the chief memorial sermon on the death of Whitefield. Wesley described Whitefield's ministry as centered on justification and new birth, the two unifying doctrines of the awakening. Calvinists were outraged, insisting that the core of Whitefield's message was grace, and therefore predestination. Wesley was closer to the mark in his depiction of Whitefield, but the sermon only added more fuel to the fire.

The Countess fired Joseph Benson from his role as tutor to her school in Trevecca due to his Wesleyan sympathies, and insisted her students oppose the *Minutes* or leave the school. This in turn led to the resignation of John Fletcher, mentor of Benson and ally of Wesley, from his position as superintendent of the school. Huntingdon and Shirley then sent a circular letter to around a hundred Calvinists throughout England to meet in Bristol at the same time as Wesley's 1771 conference. The result was a disappointment: almost no one came. Nonetheless, Walter Shirley asked to meet Wesley and his conference to discuss the issue, and those discussions resulted in the following statement by the 1771 conference:

> Whereas the Doctrinal points in the *Minutes* of a Conference held in London, August the 7th, 1770 have been understood to favour justification by works: Now the Revd. John Wesley and others assembled in Conference do declare, That we had no such meaning; and that we abhor the

---

23. Jones et al., *Elect Methodists*, 157.

The Later Controversies

doctrine of justification by works, as a most perilous and abominable doctrine.[24]

It goes on to note the 1770 *Minutes* were "not sufficiently guarded in the way they are expressed" and to affirm good works as a mark of "a real Christian believer" while "having no part in meriting or purchasing our justification..."[25] The next day Walter Shirley published his *Acknowledgement* stating he had misunderstood the *Minutes* and expressing his approval of the new 1771 statement.[26]

This should have ended the controversy but it did not. John Fletcher had been preparing a series of responses to Shirley defending the 1770 *Minutes*, and impressed by their strength of argument, Wesley wanted to rush them to publication. The result was a pamphlet war that continued from 1771 to 1777.

By this time John Fletcher (1729–85) had become Wesley's chief theological ally. Born in Switzerland, Fletcher did not pursue ministerial training there because he rejected the Reformed teaching of predestination. Coming to England in 1750, he soon became part of the Methodist movement and was ordained a priest in the Church of England in 1757. Throughout the 1760s and 1770s Fletcher was seen with John and Charles Wesley as the trio leading the Wesleyan wing of the awakening.

Fletcher's responses to Walter Shirley became known as his *First Check to Antinomiasm*, the beginning of a series of defenses of Wesleyan doctrine collectively known as the *Checks to Antinomianism*, or "Mr. Fletcher's *Checks*." These were essential reading for Wesley's Methodists on both sides of the Atlantic well into the nineteenth century.

---

24. "Annual Minutes of Some Late Conversations, 1771," *Works* 10:403.

25. Ibid.

26. McGongle, *Sufficient Saving Grace*, 277.

Fletcher was an ardent proponent of Wesley's Arminianism and his teaching on Christian perfection. While tightly reasoned and strongly argued, Fletcher's writing had an irenic nature, avoiding name-calling and exhibiting respect for opponents. This cannot be said of all the contributions to this controversy—some of the more extreme Calvinists readily engaged in denunciation, and others on both sides drifted into it from time to time.

One result of this controversy was Wesley's founding of the *Arminian Magazine* in 1778 as a counterweight to the Calvinist *Gospel Magazine*. This became a central vehicle for the publication of news, testimonies, and essays, including many of Wesley's later sermons.

RENEWAL OR SEPARATION?

In 1763, the question "What may we reasonably believe to be God's design in raising up the preachers called 'Methodists'?" was added to the published "Large" *Minutes of Several Conversations*. The answer succinctly states not only the mission of the preachers but of Wesley's movement as a whole: "To reform the nation, and in particular the Church, and to spread scriptural holiness over the land."[27] They had come to see themselves, pietist–style, as a renewal movement within the Church of England. But the relationship with the Church was always complicated. In addition to those Anglicans who believed the Church was not in need of the renewal envisioned by Wesley, the irregular methods of Methodism caused unease among many clergy who might otherwise have been supportive. Both the Wesleyan and various Calvinistic Methodist connections were in a legal gray area, where they were neither Dissenters nor part of the official structure of the Church.

27. "The Revised Disciplinary *Minutes* 1753–89," *Works* 10:845.

The Later Controversies

The existence of a separate, independently-run organization opened the door to contemplating actual separation. Wesley first faced this issue in the 1750s, when some lay preachers began offering the sacrament of the Lord's Supper in London. Charles Wesley emphatically opposed this as separation from the Church, and John found himself caught in the middle. Although the 1755 Conference at Leeds made a decision not to separate, and that lay preachers would refrain from celebrating the Lord's Supper, Charles still believed John was wavering on the issue. From John's perspective, Charles was over-reacting; his strong (Gareth Lloyd calls it "obsessive")[28] concern to maintain loyalty to the church was preventing him from understanding the complexities of the of the situation. But in 1758, John published *Reasons against a Separation from the Church of England*, a document that won his brother's approval.[29]

Yet the issue of unordained lay preachers offering the sacrament was not so easily resolved. In February, 1760 some lay preachers in Norwich took it upon themselves to administer the Lord's Supper. Once again, Charles Wesley engaged in correspondence with John accusing him of reluctance to firmly deal with this open violation of the decision of the 1755 conference. As John Tyson notes, "The Norwich affair gave Charles greater grievances against the lay preachers than he had already had, and it exacerbated his fears about the Methodists separating from the Church of England." He believed most of the lay preachers were "corrupted" and the danger of separation was immediate.[30]

---

28. Lloyd, *Charles Wesley*, 129.

29. For an extended account see Tyson, *Assist Me to Proclaim*, chapter 14; and Lloyd, *Charles Wesley*, 120–33.

30. Tyson, *Assist Me to Proclaim*, 277.

In August, 1760 the Conference in Bristol reaffirmed the Wesleyan connection's position against separation and the lay administration of the sacrament. There Charles Wesley and Howell Harris had forcefully opposed abandoning the Church, while John Wesley (according to Harris) was more reserved in his comments.

Why did John Wesley wait until the August Conference to address the issue? It may be that he was genuinely of two minds on the issue of separation. But more likely it was that he wanted time to gauge opinion among his Methodists. As Gareth Lloyd points out, John was well aware that the Norwich society contained Calvinists as well as Arminians, and the entire area had a heavily Dissenting background. The lay preachers may have been responding to public pressure in offering the sacrament. However, it soon became clear that most Methodists, especially in the London society, had no desire, much less intention, to leave the Church.[31] That knowledge may have had a moderating influence on the lay preachers at the August conference.

It is also possible that John Wesley was less strident than Charles because he wanted to not only avoid separation but also not damage the Methodist movement. To do both of these called for tact and diplomacy. It is also likely that John approached the issue more calmly because he never saw the Methodists on the brink of separation as did Charles.

But if the issue was not as serious as Charles Wesley feared, neither did it go away. As time went on the Methodists developed an increasing sense of their own ethos and identity in distinction from the Church. Charles Wesley and his many allies opposing separation continued to worry whether John would maintain his resolve to remain in the Church. In a letter written in 1772 Charles penned

31. Lloyd, *Charles Wesley*, 164–79.

this insightful observation: "All the difference betwixt my brother and me (I told him) was that my brother's first object was the Methodists, and then the church; mine was first the church, and then the Methodists. That our different judgment of persons was owing to our different temper: his all hope, and mine all fear."[32]

The source of the next major controversy over ordination was not in England but in America.[33] Methodism had begun in America in the early 1760s in Maryland and New York, when persons who had been lay preachers in Ireland continued their ministry in the colonies. Class meetings were established, societies formed, and the movement spread. All of this was occurring without John Wesley's knowledge until he received a request for assistance. In response Wesley designated America as a circuit and began sending pairs of lay preacher volunteers to oversee and guide the growing movement.

American Methodism was emerging as the political tensions between the colonies and the British government were worsening. Initially sympathetic to American complaints, Wesley changed his mind upon reading Samuel Johnson's *Taxation no Tyranny*. Wesley "extracted the chief arguments from that treatise," added an "application," and in 1775 published it as *A Calm Address to Our American Colonies*.[34] It was widely-read in England and became notorious among revolutionary circles in America. Wesley followed this in 1776 with *Some Observations on Liberty*, where

32. Tyson, *Assist Me to Proclaim*, 281.

33. For an extended account of Wesley and the American Methodists, see Heitzenrater, *Wesley and the People Called Methodists*, 288–90, 292–94, 305–6, 317–21; Collins, *John Wesley*, 210–14, 232–34; and Rack, *Reasonable Enthusiast*, 506–21.

34. "A Calm Address to Our American Colonies," *Works* (J) 11:80.

he argued that despite their claims otherwise, Americans continue to possess the same religious and civil liberties as persons in England. What they are really seeking, Wesley said, is not liberty but "independency"; they have a right to the first not the second.[35] The American claim that they have become "enslaved" is manifestly false, as a comparison to the condition of actual slaves readily reveals.[36]

By the time this second tract was published the revolution was well underway. In 1777 Wesley called for his appointed lay preachers to return to England, with only Francis Asbury deciding to remain. Wesley's tracts as well as loyalist comments from some of the departing preachers discredited Methodism in the eyes of many American patriots. Moreover, both Methodism and its Anglican parent were bereft of leadership and in disarray. Asbury, a pacifist, waited out the war in Delaware, leaving local societies and preachers to operate as they could.

The absence of ordained Anglican clergy and the inability of unordained Methodist preachers to provide the Sacraments created a crisis more severe than that faced by Methodists in England. After two years of discussion, Methodist preachers from the southern colonies met in conference at Fluvanna, Virginia, and decided to form a presbytery with the authority to ordain. As Richard Heitzenrater notes, this was "the consequence of two Wesleyan principles: the necessity of constant Communion and the prerequisite of ordination for administration of the sacrament." However, it was also "a breach of the ordered structures of the Church and represented a palpable step toward separation."[37] Asbury immediately recognized this, and opposed the action, a view confirmed by the northern

---

35. "Some Observations on Liberty," *Works* (J) 11:95.

36. Ibid., *Works* (J) 11:117.

37. Heitzenrater, *Wesley and the People Called Methodists*, 305–6.

preachers in conference the following year. In the end, the southern preachers acquiesced, and asked Asbury to write Wesley for a solution.

Wesley sought to have Methodist preachers ordained for ministry in America to no avail. With America victorious and the war ended, and finding the doors to ordination through regular channels shut, Wesley felt compelled to take a more radical step. He had been convinced for some time through the work of scholars Peter King and Edward Stillingfleet that all elders had the right to ordain. In practice, for the good order of the church, that authority was exercised only by bishops. But with regard to the Methodists Wesley was in the role of a scriptural bishop, and in America there was no longer an established Church of England. With some apparent initial reluctance yet a firm resolve, Wesley himself ordained two of his lay preachers, Thomas Vasey and Richard Whatcoat, as well as ordaining Thomas Coke, who was a priest of the Church of England, to serve as "superintendent" in America, in effect, as a bishop. The three were instructed to ordain Asbury and make him a superintendent as well.

The ordinations were discreetly performed and Charles Wesley was not notified beforehand. When he did learn of what his brother had done, some two months after the event, Charles (in Tyson's words) "vacillated between anger and sarcasm on one hand and disappointment and betrayal on the other."[38] John could insist that he was not ordaining anyone for the Church of England and was as loyal to the Church as ever, but for Charles the unauthorized act of ordination was in itself an act of separation.

For John Wesley, missional necessity always took precedence over Church order. Structure and rules were means, not ends; their purpose is always to serve the mission of

38. Tyson, *Assist Me to Proclaim*, 311.

God in the world. It would be unfair to say Charles was unconcerned about mission—after all he embraced the same irregular methods of the Methodists as did his brother. But his loyalty to the Church placed limits on what he would entertain, while for John the Methodist mission sometimes led him to take actions that went beyond those limits. In the end, after his brother's death, John Wesley would ordain lay preachers to serve in some of the remote areas of England itself, again to ensure the sacrament was readily available to persons longing for grace.

Earlier in that same year Wesley dealt with the thorny issue of the leadership of his Methodists upon his death. Unable to find a suitable successor, Wesley settled on leadership by the Conference of the People Called Methodists, consisting of one hundred of his preachers. This was set forth in the Deed of Declaration, which would take effect upon the deaths of John and Charles Wesley.[39] To some, this independent structure looked like another step toward separation from the Church.

John Wesley saw himself as loyal to the Church, but he did not believe the Church was itself loyal to its own deepest purpose. Writing in 1785, Wesley defined the universal church as everyone "in the universe whom God hath so called out of the world . . . to be 'one body', united by 'one spirit'; having 'one faith, one hope, one baptism; one God and Father of all'. . ."[40] As the congregation of believers, the church "is called 'holy' because every member thereof is holy, though in different degrees, as he that called them is holy."[41] The church, then, consists of persons either seeking holiness or growing in holiness.

---

39. Heitzenrater, *Wesley and the People Called Methodists*, 314–17.

40. "Of the Church," ¶ I.14, *Works* 3:50.

41. Ibid., ¶ III.28 *Works* 3:55–56.

Thus Wesley rejected as inadequate the typical Protestant definition found in the Articles of Religion of the Church of England that the church is where the word is rightly preached and the sacraments rightly administered. While he favored both, he recognized there are congregations with right preaching and sacraments in which people are not aiming for holiness, as well as churches that are not Protestant in which people are growing in holiness.[42]

That historically the universal church had fallen short of its calling to holiness is evident even in the apostolic church. Infected by "the mystery of iniquity," the early church was plagued by the favoring of one group over another, tolerance of overt sin, the desire for money or possessions, and lack of forbearance for others due to strong insistence on one's own opinions.[43] When Christianity became the official religion of the Roman Empire, it received riches and power, and "a grand blow was struck at the very root of that humble, gentle, patient love, which is . . . the whole essence of true religion."[44] This has been the deplorable condition of the church ever since.

Methodism was intended to renew the church in holiness, but it too had been infected by these things, most especially the desire for wealth. "The Methodists," Wesley wrote in 1789, "grow more and more self indulgent, because they *grow rich*,[45] and "are deplorably wanting in the practice of Christian self denial."[46] There was a growing need for Methodists themselves to return to their roots if they were to be a leaven in the Church of England.

---

42. Ibid., ¶ I.18, *Works* 3:52.
43. "The Mystery of Iniquity," ¶ 14–21, 2:456–60.
44. Ibid., ¶ 27, *Works* 2:462–63.
45. "Causes of the Inefficacy of Christianity," ¶ 16, *Works* 4:95.
46. Ibid., ¶ 17, *Works* 4:95–96.

But for those Methodists who were growing in holiness, and impatient for change in the Church, Wesley warned that separation was not the answer. In the "Large" *Minutes* from the early 1770s Wesley stated

> We are not Seceders, nor do we bear any resemblance to them. We set out upon quite opposite principles. The Seceders laid the very foundation of their work in judging and condemning *others*. We laid the foundation of our work in judging and condemning ourselves.[47]

The renewal of the Church occurs not through condemnation of others but through one's own repentance.

In his 1786 sermon "On Schism" Wesley laid out in more detail as to why this is the case. While "schism" in scripture normally means internal disunity within a church, Wesley allowed that its meaning may be extended to separation from a church. Schism "in this sense," he argues, "is both evil in itself, and productive of evil consequences."[48] It is evil in itself because separation "from a body of living Christians with whom we were before united is a grievous breach of the law of love." While the "pretenses for separation may be innumerable," the "want of love is always the real cause . . ."[49] It produces evil consequences in that it "opens a door to all unkind tempers, both in ourselves and others. It leads directly to a whole chain of evil surmisings, to severe and uncharitable judging of each other." This may ultimately "issue in bitterness, malice, and settled hatred; creating a present hell wherever they are found, as a prelude the hell eternal."[50]

---

47. "The Revised Disciplinary *Minutes*, 1753–89," *Works* 10:891.
48. "On Schism," ¶ 10, *Works* 3:64.
49. Ibid., ¶ 11, *Works* 3:64.
50. Ibid., ¶ 12, *Works* 3:65.

The Later Controversies

Is separation ever warranted? Yes, said Wesley, but only when one "cannot continue therein with a clear conscience" or "without sin." If such is the case "you could not be blamed for separating from that society."[51]

Wesley's argument against separation was ultimately on the same ground as his definition of the church: the priority of love, of holiness of heart and life. This concern was also what was at stake in his arguments with the perfectionists in his own movement and the Calvinists without. Methodism at its very center was about proclaiming the message of God's love to all, and the intent of God to enable us to be renewed in that divine image. Wesley had devoted his life to this mission, and he would not compromise it, even if he had to violate the order and norms of the Church of England.

DISCUSSION QUESTIONS

1. How was Christian perfection misunderstood by the followers of Maxfield and Bell? How did Wesley respond?
2. How and why did John and Charles Wesley disagree about Christian perfection?
3. What is "antinomianism" and why is it a danger to salvation as Wesley understood it?
4. Why was John Wesley opposed to separation from the Church of England?
5. How did Wesley justify his ordinations of Vasey, Whatcoat, and Coke for America?
6. For John Wesley, what was the nature and purpose of the church?

---

51. Ibid., ¶ 17, *Works* 3:66–7.

10

RENEWING THE FACE OF THE EARTH

THE PATTERN OF RELIGIOUS AWAKENINGS

While large-scale religious awakenings, or revivals of religion, necessarily involve human agents, they are fundamentally works of God. Their public face is usually persons preaching to large crowds of listeners, both within and without church buildings. The eighteenth-century awakening was certainly exemplary in this regard. But decades of experience had provided Wesley with deeper insight into the nature of awakenings. This he shared in his 1783 sermon "The General Spread of the Gospel," and his depiction of awakenings there challenges many popular assumptions, both then and now.

The question Wesley sought to address in this sermon was, given the deplorable state of humanity throughout the world due to the dominance of sin and lack of holiness, how can God be both all-powerful and good? His answer was "that things will not always be so," that through Jesus Christ, God will redeem the world, such that the "loving knowledge of God, producing uniform, uninterrupted holiness and happiness, shall cover the earth, shall fill every soul of man."[1] Here one common assumption about awakenings was already challenged. Many understand revivals of religion to be focused on conversion, especially justification, with the goal of saving persons from eternal damnation. In Wesley's view, justification may be the initial emphasis, but the ultimate goal is sanctification; and while the focus is on personal salvation, the result is the spreading of holiness throughout the earth.

But how do we get from such a seemingly hopeless condition of the world, which afflicts the church as much as those outside of it, to the renewal of the world in holiness? It will be by the power of God, Wesley argued, in which God will continue to work in the same manner as God has been working. Wesley described how God had worked thus far in this way: "Generally when these truths—justification by faith in particular—were declared in any large town, after a few days or weeks there came suddenly on the great congregation . . . a violent and impetuous power," which "frequently continued, with shorter or longer intervals, for several weeks or months." But then, Wesley continued, "it gradually subsided, and then the work of God was carried on by gentle degrees . . ."[2]

Many observers would conclude that when there were no longer manifestations of that "violent and impetuous power" the awakening had ceased. Wesley saw instead that the work of God had just begun. Preaching continued, class meetings were held, testimonies were given, people

1. "The General Spread of the Gospel," ¶ 8, *Works* 2:63.
2. Ibid., ¶ 15, *Works* 2:491–92.

witnessed to their friends, all of which were a continuation of the awakening in less dramatic but nonetheless real and effectual ways. Based on this pattern of divine activity, in envisioning how God will work in the future Wesley predicted

> At the first breaking out of his work in this or that place there may be a shower, a torrent of grace. . . . But in general it seems the kingdom of God will not "come with observation" but will silently increase wherever it is set up, and spread from heart to heart, from house to house, from town to town, from one kingdom to another.[3]

This understanding of the nature and progress of an awakening as both sudden and gentle is analogous to Wesley's description of the way of salvation as both instantaneous and gradual.

This is not the only pattern of divine activity Wesley saw in the awakening. He also predicted "God will observe the same order" of human response "which he hath done from the beginning of Christianity." They shall come to know God "not from the greatest to the least (this is that wisdom of the world which is foolishness with God) but 'from the least to the greatest.'" "Before the end," Wesley said, "even the rich shall enter the kingdom of God," together with "the great, the noble, the honourable; yea the rulers, princes, the kings of the earth." Then at the end will be "all the wise and learned, the men of genius, the philosophers," who "will be convinced they are fools; will 'be converted and become as little children and enter into the kingdom of God.'"[4] This radically inverted the widespread assumption that piety and morality are more likely to be found among

---

3. Ibid., ¶ 17, *Works* 2:493.
4. Ibid., ¶ 19, *Works* 2:493–94.

the "better" classes. Both scripture and experience taught Wesley otherwise.

Wesley also had a more expansive vision of the extent of the awakening than many of his Protestant contemporaries, who tended to limit its effects to Protestant churches. While Wesley agreed that the awakening emerged within Protestantism and would initially spread through those churches, he fully expected it would eventually encompass Roman Catholic and Eastern Orthodox churches as well.[5] God intends to renew the universal church, and for Wesley that included the non-Protestants.

Finally, Wesley had a more thoroughgoing vision of the change an awakening would bring in the life of the church. Certainly everyone involved in leading the awakening believed the new birth had an impact on how one would subsequently live. But for Wesley the culmination of the awakening, when the entire church is renewed in holiness, would be nothing less than a purer manifestation of the church depicted in Acts 2. It is then that the "Grand Pentecost" will have "fully come," and devout persons in all nations "shall 'all be filled with the Holy Ghost.'" They will live according to apostolic doctrine, have fellowship with one another, partake of the Lord's Supper, and lead lives of prayer. Being now of "one heart and soul," the consequence of this renewal in holiness "will be the same as it was in the beginning of the Christian church." No one will say "the things which he possesses is his own, but they will have all things in common." As in Acts 2, lands and houses will be sold to provide for everyone as they have need. "All their desires, meantime, and passions, and tempers will be cast in one mould, while all are doing the will of God on earth as it is done in heaven."[6]

5. Ibid., ¶ 17–18, *Works* 2:493.
6. Ibid., ¶ 20, *Works* 2:494–95.

Now it is fair to say Wesley never saw churches who actually lived in accordance with this radical vision. But if the goal of salvation is perfection in love, and that goal became realized throughout the universal church, it necessarily would have a radical effect on how Christians relate to one another. Even a church in which persons were either seeking or growing in holiness would be a community far different from the typical Anglican church of Wesley's day, or many of the churches in our own.

In the later years of his ministry Wesley realized that his most pressing problem was not the lack of churches renewed in holiness but that his Methodists, who he saw as one of God's prime instruments of renewal, were themselves becoming ensnared in the pursuit of possessions and wealth. While this had been a concern of his all along, Wesley now doubled down with series of sermons. In "On God's Vineyard" (1787), "On Riches" (1788), "Causes of the Inefficacy of Christianity" (1789), and "The Danger of Increasing Riches" (1790) Wesley called the Methodists back to self-denial and holiness. Wealth, he argued, can damage our relationship with God through illusions of self-sufficiency, and the pursuit of it can undermine our generosity toward others. This was no small issue for Wesley and it certainly placed a cloud over his grand vision of a church renewed in holiness.

Yet Wesley's hope was not ultimately in humanity but in the grace of God. In the "General Spread of the Gospel" Wesley noted that while there may "be a great shaking . . . I cannot induce myself to think that God has wrought so glorious a work as to let it sink and die away in a few years." "No," he added, "I trust this is only the beginning of a far greater work—the dawn of 'the latter day glory.'"[7] Indeed,

---

7. Ibid., ¶ 16, *Works* 2:493.

"unprejudiced persons may see with their eyes that he is already renewing the face of the earth."[8]

For Wesley, it was the lack of holiness in the church that was the chief impediment to the reception of the gospel by non-Christians. But once there is a renewed church with that "grand stumbling-block being thus happily removed out of the way, namely, the lives of Christians," those outside the church "will look upon them with other eyes, and begin to give attention to their words."[9] The credibility of the gospel rests not on logical argumentation or persuasive speech but on its effects seen in the lives of Christians and in Christian communities. Wesley believed the renewal of the church in holiness is the necessary precondition for persons in all nations to believe the good news of Jesus Christ and receive the new life he offers. And that in turn ushers in the kingdom of God itself, when the will of God will indeed be done on earth as it is in heaven, and the whole creation will manifest the love of God.

A CATHOLIC SPIRIT

Historically religious awakenings are highly contentious events. While they can knit together persons across theological traditions, they can also split denominations into opponents and proponents. The initial unity in an awakening can be shaken by the re-emergence of theological differences, as it did between the Moravians, Calvinists, and Wesleyans in the eighteenth-century. The ensuing conflicts can not only challenge civility but love itself. Given that Wesley believed the whole point of salvation was to enable persons to love God and others as they are loved by God,

---

8. Ibid., ¶ 27, *Works* 2:499.
9. Ibid., ¶ 21, *Works* 2:495.

he early on gave attention to the problem of Christian unity among diverse theological and denominational traditions.

Wesley addressed the issue first in 1742 in "The Character of a Methodist" (which was primarily a description of Christian perfection, although he did not there use the term) and more fully in his 1755 sermon "Catholic Spirit." This sermon, says Albert Outler, "is a charter for a distinctive sort of doctrinal pluralism—one that stands at an equal distance from dogmatism on the one extreme and indifferentism on the other.""[10] It is premised on a distinction, common in Anglican circles of that day, between "essentials" and "opinions," but these were developed by Wesley in new and significant ways.

The sermon was based on an interchange in 2 Kings 10:15 in which Jehu asks Jehonadab, "Is thine heart right, as my heart is with thy heart?" to which Jehonadab answered, "It is. If it be, give me thine hand."[11] What does it mean for a heart to be "right?" Wesley noted that this question was not an "inquiry concerning Jehonadab's opinions,[12] nor as to his "mode of worship."[13] As Rupert Davies notes, here by "opinion" Wesley meant the "considered and deliberate convictions on matters of faith and practice held by churches and individuals, which do not affect fundamental matters of faith."[14]

That Christians will have various and conflicting opinions is an inevitable result of the human condition. We will not "see all things alike," Wesley argued, because our "present weakness and shortness of human understanding"

10. Outler, "Catholic Spirit," in *Works* 2:80.
11. "Catholic Spirit," *Works* 2:81.
12. Ibid., ¶ I. l, *Works* 2:82.
13. Ibid., ¶ I. 7, *Works* 2:85.
14. Rupert E. Davies, "The Character of a Methodist: An Introductory Comment," in *Works* 9:31.

ensures we "will be of several minds, in religion as well as in common life."[15] Moreover, while we believe every opinion we hold is true ("for to believe any opinion is not true is the same thing as not to hold it"), we can be certain that in some things we are mistaken, even though we do not know where those mistakes lie.[16]

With regard to worship, Wesley observed that "as long as there are various opinions there will be various ways of worshipping God; seeing a variety of opinions necessarily implies a variety of practice."[17] Therefore each person must "act as each is fully persuaded in his own mind." Wesley may "believe the episcopal form of government to be scriptural and apostolical," while others believe that of "the presbyterian or independent" polity. Wesley might affirm infant baptism; others in good faith may disagree.[18] Thus a wise person "will allow others the same liberty of thinking which he desires they should allow him; and will no more insist on their embracing his opinions than he would have them to insist on embracing theirs."[19] As Wesley wrote in "The Character of a Methodist," "But as to all opinions which do not strike at the root of Christianity, we 'think and let think.'"[20]

Clearly implied by this statement is that there *are* opinions that strike at the root of Christianity, or to put it more positively, there are essentials that must be affirmed. But what essentials? The obvious problem is what Wesley might have called an essential—say, the doctrine of the Trinity—an Arian would not. Or what others would have

15. "Catholic Spirit," ¶ I. 4, *Works* 2:83–84.
16. Ibid.
17. Ibid., ¶ I. 8, *Works* 2:85.
18. Ibid., ¶ II. 2, *Works* 2:89–90.
19. Ibid., ¶ I .6, *Works* 2:84.
20. "The Character of a Methodist," ¶ 1, *Works* 9:34.

claimed to be essential to the gospel, such as predestination was for a number of Calvinists, Wesley would have called an opinion. Wesley did not provide a single, definitive list of essentials, but seemed confident that scripture and ecumenical tradition was sufficient to determine what is and is not.

When he did list beliefs that are common to all Christians, he tended to only mention those pertinent to the issue at hand. Frequently, of course, he mentioned original sin, justification, and sanctification as among them, while recognizing the way in which each was understood varied from tradition to tradition. He also on many occasions affirmed as necessary belief in a Christianly-described God. For example, in his 1777 sermon "On the Trinity" Wesley insisted "the knowledge of the Three-One God is interwoven with all true Christian faith, with all vital religion." The reason was not that Christians need correct concepts but that salvation itself presupposes the work of a trinitarian God. Thus in justification "the Holy Ghost witnesses that God the Father has accepted" us "through the merits of God the Son." To be a Christian necessitated at least an implicit trinitarianism, and Wesley simply did "not see how it is possible for any to have vital religion who denies that these three are one."[21]

Now for some important distinctions. Wesley was quite clear that he was not calling for belief in any particular explanation of the Trinity—"it is the *substance* of the doctrine" that matters "not the philosophical *illustrations* of it."[22] Similarly, Wesley elsewhere stated that conflict between Christians is often not only over opinions but preferred terminology; in "The Lord Our Righteousness" he argued that "the children of God . . . so vehemently contend

21. "On the Trinity," ¶ 17, *Works* 2:385.
22. Ibid., ¶ 3, *Works* 2:376–77.

with each other" due to "their not understanding one another, joined with too keen an attachment to their *opinions* and particular modes of *expression*."[23]

In addition to setting aside certain formulations and expressions as non-essential, he was also not calling upon persons to believe any particular explanation of the Trinity. We "believe many things which" we "cannot comprehend,"[24] he argued; we can believe there is a sun over our heads without any understanding of how it occurs. Likewise, we can believe the fact of the incarnation while knowing nothing of the *manner* in which the Son of God became flesh.[25] So it is with the Trinity: *that* God is triune has been revealed to us; the *manner* has not.[26]

To return to "Catholic Spirit," here too Wesley described essential beliefs as necessarily interwoven with the heart and life in his depiction of a "heart right with God." He began by asking, "Dost thou believe his being, and his perfections? His eternity, immensity, wisdom, power; his justice, mercy, and truth?" But these attributes were more than intellectual concepts for Wesley, they were experienced realities that impact life: "Hast thou a divine evidence, a supernatural conviction, of the things of God? Dost thou 'walk by faith, not by sight'?"[27] Do you *know* this God?

The same is true of God the Son: "Dost thou believe in the Lord Jesus Christ . . .? Is he 'revealed in' thy soul? Dost thou 'know Jesus Christ and him crucified'? Dost he 'dwell in thee, and thou in him'?[28] What we know and

---

23. "The Lord Our Righteousness," ¶ 6, *Works* 1:452.
24. "On the Trinity," ¶ 6, *Works* 2:379.
25. Ibid., ¶ 14, *Works* 2:384.
26. Ibid., ¶ 15, *Works* 2:384.
27. "Catholic Spirit," ¶ I.12, *Works* 2:87.
28. Ibid., ¶ I. 13, *Works* 2:87.

who we know is inextricably bound together in Christian experience.

Wesley then continued his depiction of a heart right with God by asking "Dost thou love God," do you seek to do God's will, and does your love for God lead you to serve God?[29] Finally, he asked, "Is thy heart right toward thy neighbor," and "Do you show your love by your works?"[30] If all of this is the case, then one's heart is indeed right with God.

If your heart is right with God as my heart, said Wesley, then "give me thine hand."[31] This means not to adopt my opinions or modes of worship but to "love me," "commend me to God in all thy prayers," "provoke me to love and to good works," and "love me not in word only, but in deed and in truth."[32]

In emphasizing that opinions should not be barriers to Christian love and unity, Wesley was not setting them aside as inconsequential. It would have been odd for him to do so, given his own controversies with the Moravians and Calvinists, among others. There were, he believed, important, even vital issues at stake. Here may be Wesley's most important insight in this sermon: while opinions are not essentials of the faith, that does not mean they are unimportant. Wesley and the Calvinists should vigorously debate predestination and prevenient grace as matters of great significance; but that disagreement, however intense, should not break the bonds of Christian love nor lead persons on one side to claim those on the other are not Christians.

In fact, Wesley took this a step further: he insisted that on some matters it was *necessary* to have an opinion,

---

29. Ibid., ¶ I. 14–16, *Works* 2:88.
30. Ibid., ¶ I. 17–18, *Works* 2:89.
31. Ibid., ¶ II. 1, *Works* 2:89.
32. Ibid., ¶ II. 3–7, *Works* 2:90–92.

even if it disagreed with other Christians. A "catholic spirit is not *speculative latitudinarianism*," an "indifference to all opinions"; nor is it "any kind of *practical latitudinarianism*," an "indifference as to public worship or as to the outward manner of performing it."[33] It really does matter whether one believes infants are proper recipients of baptism, or saving grace is only given to the predestined elect. Thus a person "of a truly catholic spirit has not now his religion to seek. He is fixed as the sun in his judgment concerning the main branches of Christian doctrine." While always open to argument, a person of catholic spirit does "not halt between two opinions, nor vainly endeavor to blend them into one."[34] A catholic spirit adopts and lives in accordance with those opinions believed most faithful to scripture, while accepting that other, equally faithful Christians may hold different opinions.

So it was not a belief that opinions are insignificant that governed Wesley's understanding of a catholic spirit, but the pre-eminence of love. If that was the point of salvation, then nothing else, however important in itself, could be permitted to be a barrier to love. As Wesley wrote in 1746

> For how far is love, even with many wrong opinions, to be preferred before truth itself without love? We may die without the knowledge of many truths and yet be carried into Abraham's bosom. But if we die without love, what will knowledge avail? . . . The God of love forbid we should ever make the trial! May he prepare us for the knowledge of all truth, by filling our hearts with all his love, and with all joy and peace in believing.[35]

33. Ibid., ¶ III. 1–2, *Works* 2:92–93.

34. Ibid., ¶ III. 1, *Works* 2:93.

35. "The Preface, Sermons on Several Occasions," ¶ 10, *Works* 1:107.

THE NEW CREATION

In many sermons written during the last decade of his life Wesley sought to place the way of salvation within the larger framework of the entire work of God, from creation to new creation. From this perspective holiness of heart and life is the life of the coming kingdom of God in the present; the soteriological "already" to the eschatological "not yet." It is love now governing the heart and life as we await the time when God's love shall fill the entire world.

Whenever Wesley spoke of the age to come it had implications for the present age. When Wesley read in Romans 8:22 that "The whole creation groaneth together, and travaileth together in pain until now,"[36] he understood it as a promise that "the brute creation" would not "always remain in this deplorable condition." The entire "animated creation" awaits "that final 'manifestation of the sons of God': in which 'they themselves also shall be delivered' (not by annihilation: annihilation is not deliverance) 'from the' present 'bondage of corruption, into' a measure of 'the glorious liberty of the children of God.'"[37] That the promise is for the deliverance of this present creation rather than its annihilation placed a value on the created order in the present, among other things implying for Wesley a need for compassionate care of animals, especially those that were domesticated,[38] and for us today care for the larger environment as well.

This was underscored by Wesley's vision of the new creation not simply as a recovery of Edenic paradise but something far beyond it in goodness and love. Thus in the new creation, "the whole brute creation will then undoubtably be restored, not only to the vigour, strength,

---

36. "The General Deliverance," ¶ I. 6, *Works* 3:442.
37. Ibid., ¶ III. 1, *Works* 2:445.
38. Ibid., ¶ II. 6, *Works* 2:444-45.

and swiftness which they had at their creation, but to a far higher degree of each than they ever enjoyed." Likewise their understanding and "whatever affections they had in the garden of Eden will be restored with vast increase" in such a manner as we presently are unable to comprehend.[39] This speaks of a care, even love, for all creatures by their Creator that those of us created in that Creator's image are called to emulate.

Wesley's central concern was human salvation, and as we saw in chapter 6, he had this same vision of the new creation as greater than the original in his theology of Christian perfection. While Adam and Eve knew the love of God, they did not know the depth of that love in the cross of Jesus Christ. Because we do, in being restored to the image of God we are able to attain a depth of love in our own hearts and lives not possible for our first parents. Our thus imaging of God's love in Christ is not only for the age to come, but is an eschatological reality within the present age.

Wesley frequently used eschatological language to describe aspects of the way of salvation. In "The Way to the Kingdom" he related holiness and happiness to the kingdom of God in that "it is the immediate fruit of God reigning in the soul." As soon as God "takes unto himself his mighty power, and sets up his throne in our hearts," we "are instantly filled with this 'righteousness, and peace, and joy in the Holy Ghost.'" With regard to its synonym the "kingdom of heaven," Wesley saw the new birth as "(in degree) heaven opened in the soul."[40] Thus the life of the age to come is already a reality in the hearts and lives of believers. Even "if the harvest is not yet," Wesley said, we can nonetheless be part of its "first fruits."[41]

39. Ibid., III. 3, *Works* 2:446.
40. "The Way to the Kingdom," ¶ I. 12, *Works* 1:244.
41. "Upon Our Lord's Sermon on the Mount, II," ¶ III.18 *Works* 1:508–9.

He similarly applied eschatological language to faith. Knowing the love of God through Christ was variously called by Wesley "a foretaste of heaven,"[42] "heaven opened in the soul,"[43] and tasting the powers of the world to come.[44] Faith enables us to know in the present the love that will be fully manifest in the age to come, thereby enabling it to come to birth in our hearts.

From this perspective Wesley understood his Methodist connection to be eschatological yeast that would renew the church in holiness and live out in the present the life of the age to come. It would be a living witness to the coming reality, both in its own life together and as, through its actions, it gave the world a genuine foretaste of that love which triumphs over sin and suffering.

DISCUSSION QUESTIONS

1. As a leader in a large-scale Christian awakening, what patterns did Wesley see? Did his observations surprise you, and if so, why?

2. Some might argue that Christians should set aside their differences in order to unify, while others insist there can be no unity without prior agreement on beliefs and practices. How would Wesley respond?

3. In what ways is the life of the coming new creation already potentially present today? What aspects of the new creation await the return of Jesus Christ?

---

42. "The Important Question," ¶ III. 14, *Works* 3:197.

43. "Spiritual Worship," ¶ II. 5, *Works* 3:96.

44. "The Way to the Kingdom," ¶ II. 10, *Works* 1:223, and "Self-Denial," ¶ II. 5, *Works* 2:246–7.

Conclusion

THE TRIUMPH OF LOVE

Wesley's vision of a new creation filled with the love of God is a fitting outcome of his theology. From 1725 on he was committed to holiness of heart and life as the content and goal of salvation; now, near the end of his life, he extended renewal in love from the hearts of humans to the entirety of creation. This was one of the last of the many insights Wesley gained throughout his life and ministry.

His fundamental insight, that governed all the rest, was that salvation is all about our renewal in love, our being restored to the image of God. Without this holiness of heart and life we are neither truly happy nor truly Christian. In saying this Wesley corrected the pervasive notion that Christian salvation is solely about our post-mortem destiny, insisting instead it is about receiving a new life in the present, one that lasts through all eternity. He also redirected us from our tendency to find meaning in life, and our own self-worth, through our accomplishments, material success, or esteem from others. The issue is not what have we done but who we are: are we persons motivated by acquiring things or gaining praise, for example, or by love for God and neighbor? Wesley insisted that the meaning of life is found in the intentions of our Creator who gave us life, and until we are once again in the image in which we were created we can never really be happy or fulfilled.

Wesley became convinced that becoming persons who mirror God's love was the goal of the Christian life when he was at Oxford in 1725. What he struggled with was how to attain the goal. He eventually realized, as had Augustine and Martin Luther before him, that our fallen condition inevitably subverts even our best efforts. The common belief in contemporary American culture that there is a wonderful self inside of us waiting to be actualized would be considered hopelessly naive by Wesley. The actual evidence of both human history and our own lives and relationships stand as witness against it. We have a problem we ourselves cannot solve.

Salvation, he learned in 1738, comes from outside of ourselves, as a free gift of God, given through the cross of Jesus Christ and actualized in our lives by the Holy Spirit. This grace is received by faith, and available to everyone. Salvation, defined as eternal destiny, is still widely believed in American society as the reward for those who have been "good," or at least good enough. But Wesley saw that the very seeking to earn divine approval nurtures within us dispositions of the heart that salvation aims to replace. Our relationship to God is radically changed when we move from seeking to earn God's love to gratefully receiving it as a gift. As a result, new motivations and desires are then born in the heart that put us on the road to ever-increasing holiness.

That our renewal in love is a work of divine power led Wesley to develop a more dynamic theology of the Holy Spirit than his Protestant predecessors. Grace for Wesley was much more than divine favor, which then and now is often construed in such a way as to leave persons fundamentally unchanged rather than as entry into a transformative relationship with God. Grace at its heart *is* the power of the Holy Spirit; thus, we can approach God with an expectant, although not a presumptive, faith.

Wesley is also exceptionally helpful in showing us where we normally encounter this transforming power. Although by no means denying miracles or other extraordinary works of God, Wesley cautioned us not to make them our focus. Even more he warned against the uncritical identification of God with intense feelings or strong inclinations. Instead, Wesley advised a faithful attention to those means of grace where God has promised to meet us: prayer, fasting, Christian conference, reading scripture, care for the neighbor, and regular attendance at worship and participation in the Lord's Supper. It is in the means of grace we encounter the God revealed in Jesus Christ, and correct our tendency to turn God into a divinity of our own making.

Wesley was also aware that our using these means of grace can become routine, or even a way to earn God's approval. This danger of formalism is tied to our being almost insensibly drawn away from God, not only through temptation but by the sheer business of life. It was this concern Wesley's highly developed system of spiritual discipline and weekly meetings were designed to address. Through these, faith was nurtured and focus maintained on God and the neighbor. Wesley's approach challenges the pervasive privatization of religion in American culture today. Wesley considered solitary religion a recipe for disaster; he did not see how persons could grow in faith and love apart from community and discipline.

Wesley's strong emphasis on the work of the Holy Spirit gave his theology a trinitarian shape. While many of his theologically orthodox contemporaries sought to defend the logical coherence of the doctrine of the Trinity against a growing number of deist, unitarian, and Arian critics, Wesley was inviting persons to experience the work of the triune God in their own lives. Wesley's theology has a trinitarian substructure that sustains the whole; it is most visible in Wesley's frequent presentation of the heart of divine activity as God's love for us revealed in the cross of Jesus Christ, and God's bringing that love to birth within us through the power of the Holy Spirit.

It was also his dynamic understanding of the Spirit that enabled Wesley to have an optimism of grace. As we have said, there is no way to get from a Protestant doctrine of original sin to attaining Christian perfection in this life except through a strong belief in the transforming work of the Spirit. That said, Wesley's optimism of grace never led him to forget that we are presently living in this age, not the age to come. In eschatological terms, Wesley's more expansive sense of the "already" of the kingdom of God remains in tension with the "not yet"; expectant hope is always tempered by humble realism. Even those who attain Christian perfection are reminded of their continual need for repentance, as involuntary transgressions remain.

The good news of God's love for us in Jesus Christ and the promise of our renewal in love through the Holy Spirit was Wesley's message to the world, and enabling persons to receive that promise and grow in that love was the purpose

The Triumph of Love

of the discipline and societies of his Methodism. Even on his deathbed this concern was paramount. There Wesley asked "Where is my sermon on The Love of God? Take it and spread it abroad; give it to everyone." Ten thousand copies of "God's Love to Fallen Man" were then printed and given away.[1]

Commenting on 1 John 4:19 ("We love him, because he first loved us") Wesley wrote, "This is the sum of all religion, the genuine model of Christianity. None can say more: why should any one say less..."[2] Wesley believed that this love of God will triumph in the end, and it is this same love that seeks to triumph even now, in every human heart.

DISCUSSION QUESTIONS

1. If someone asked you to name the most important emphases in Wesley's theology and practice, what would they be?
2. What do you see as some important contributions Wesley can make to Christian life and mission today?

---

1. Albert C. Outler, "Introductory Comment" to "God's Love to Fallen Man," in *Works* 2:422.
2. *Explanatory Notes on the New Testament*, 1 John 4:19.

BIBLIOGRAPHY

Bangs, Carl. *Arminius: A Study in the Dutch Reformation*. Nashville: Abingdon, 1971.
Best, Gary. *Charles Wesley: A Biography*. London: Epworth, 2006.
Borgen, Ole E. *John Wesley on the Sacraments*. Nashville: Abingdon, 1972.
Brendlinger, Irv A. *Social Justice through the Eyes of Wesley: John Wesley's Theological Challenge to Slavery*. Guelph, ON: Joshua Press, 2006.
Brian, Rustin E. *Jacob Arminius: The Man from Oudewater*. Eugene, OR: Cascade, 2015.
Brown, Dale W. *Understanding Pietism*. Rev. ed. Nappanee, IN: Evangel, 1996.
Brown, Earl Kent. *Women of Mr. Wesley's Methodism*. Lewiston, NY: E. Mellen, 1982.
Burdon, Adrian. *Authority and Order: John Wesley and His Preachers*. Aldershot, UK: Ashgate, 2005.
Campbell, Ted A. "Conversion and Baptism in Wesleyan Spirituality." In *Conversion in the Wesleyan Tradition*, edited by Kenneth J. Collins and John H. Tyson, 160–74. Nashville: Abingdon, 2001.
Cannon, William R. *The Theology of John Wesley, with Special Reference to the Doctrine of Justification*. 1946. Reprint, Lanham, MD: University Press of America, 1984.
Cell, George C. *The Rediscovery of John Wesley*. 1935. Reprint, Lanham MD: University Press of America, 1984.
Chilcote, Paul Wesley. *John Wesley and the Women Preachers of Early Methodism*. Metuchen, NJ: Scarecrow, 1991.
Clapper, Gregory S. *John Wesley on Religious Affections*. Metuchen, NJ: Scarecrow, 1989.

Bibliography

Collins, Kenneth J. *John Wesley: A Theological Journey*. Nashville: Abingdon, 2003.

———. *The Theology of John Wesley*. Nashville: Abingdon, 2007.

Cracknell, Kenneth, and Susan J. White. *An Introduction to World Methodism*. Cambridge: Cambridge University Press, 2005.

Danker, Ryan Nicholas. *Wesley and the Anglicans: Political Division in Early Evangelicalism*. Downers Grove, IL: IVP Academic, 2016.

Dieter, Melvin Easterday. *The Holiness Revival of the Nineteenth Century*. 2nd ed. Lanham, MD: Scarecrow, 1996.

Freeman, Arthur J. *An Ecumenical Theology of the Heart: The Theology of Count Nicholas Ludwig von Zinzendorf*. Bethlehem, PA: Moravian Church in America, 1998.

Hammond, Geordan. *John Wesley in America: Restoring Primitive Christianity*. New York: Oxford University Press, 2014.

Harding, Alan. *The Countess of Huntingdon's Connexion: A Sect in Action*. Oxford: Oxford University Press, 2003.

———. *Selena, Countess of Huntingdon*. London: Epworth, 2008.

Heitzenrater, Richard P. *Wesley and the People Called Methodists*. 2nd ed. Nashville: Abingdon, 2013.

Holland, Bernard. *Baptism in Early Methodism*. London: Epworth, 1970.

Hollenweger, Walter J. *Pentecostalism: Origin and Developments Worldwide*. Peabody, MA: Hendrickson, 1997.

Jones, David Ceri, et al. *The Elect Methodists: Calvinistic Methodism in England and Wales, 1735–1811*. Cardiff: University of Wales Press, 2012.

Khoo, Lorna Lock-Nah. *Wesleyan Eucharistic Spirituality: Its Nature, Sources, and Future*. Adelaide, SA: ATF Press, 2005.

Kidd, Thomas S. *George Whitefield: America's Spiritual Founding Father*. New Haven: Yale University Press, 2014.

Kisker, Scott Thomas. *Foundation for Revival: Anthony Horneck, the Religious Societies, and the Construction of an Anglican Pietism*. Lanham, MD: Scarecrow, 2008.

Knight, Henry H. III. *Anticipating Heaven Below: Optimism of Grace from Wesley to the Pentecostals*. Eugene, OR: Cascade, 2014.

———, ed. *From Aldersgate to Azusa Street*. Eugene, OR: Pickwick, 2010.

———. *The Presence of God in the Christian Life*. Metuchen, NJ: Scarecrow, 1992.

Lambert, Frank. *"Pedlar in Divinity": George Whitefield and the Transatlantic Revivals, 1737–1770*. Princeton: Princeton University Press, 1993.

Bibliography

Lewis, A. J. *Zinzendorf, the Ecumenical Pioneer: A Study in the Moravian Contribution to Christian Ministry and Unity*. London: SCM, 1962.

Lindberg, Carter. *The Pietist Theologians*. Hoboken, NJ: Wiley-Blackwell, 2004.

Lindstrom, Harold. *Wesley and Sanctification: A Study in the Doctrine of Salvation*. 1950. Reprint, Grand Rapids: Francis Asbury, 1982.

Lloyd, Gareth. *Charles Wesley and the Struggle for Methodist Identity*. Oxford: Oxford University Press, 2007.

Macquiban, Tim. "Friends of All? The Wesleyan Response to Urban Poverty in Britain and Ireland, 1785–1840." In *The Poor and the People Called Methodists*, edited by Richard P. Heitzenrater, 131–60. Nashville: Kingswood, 2002.

Madden, Deborah. *"A Cheap, Safe and Natural Medicine": Religion, Medicine and Culture in John Wesley's Primitive Physic*. Amsterdam: Rodopi, 2007.

———. "Saving Souls and Saving Lives: John Wesley's 'Inward and Outward Health.'" In *Inward and Outward Health: John Wesley's Holistic Concept of Medical Science, the Environment and Holy Living*, edited by Deborah Madden, 1–14. London: Epworth, 2008.

Maddox, Randy L. *Responsible Grace: John Wesley's Practical Theology*. Nashville: Kingswood, 1994.

———. "An Untapped Inheritance: American Methodism and Wesley's Practical Theology." In *Doctrines and Discipline*, edited by Dennis M. Campbell et al., 19–52. Nashville: Abingdon, 1999.

Martin, David. *Pentecostalism: The World Their Parish*. Oxford: Blackwell, 2002.

McGonigle, Herbert. *Sufficient Saving Grace: John Wesley's Evangelical Arminianism*. Carlisle, UK: Paternoster, 2001.

Meeks, M. Douglas, ed. *The Portion of the Poor: Good News to the Poor in the Wesleyan Tradition*. Nashville: Kingswood, 1995.

Newton, John A. *Susanna Wesley and the Puritan Tradition in Methodism*. 2nd ed. London: Epworth, 2005.

Noll, Mark A. *The Rise of Evangelicalism: The Age of Edwards, Whitefield and the Wesleys*. Downers Grove, IL: InterVarsity, 2003.

Olson, Roger E. *Arminian Theology: Myths and Realities*. Downers Grove, IL: InterVarsity, 2006.

Olson, Roger E., and Christian T. Collins Winn. *Reclaiming Pietism: Retrieving an Evangelical Tradition*. Grand Rapids: Eerdmans, 2015.

Bibliography

Outler, Albert C., ed. *John Wesley*. Oxford: Oxford University Press, 1964.

Outler, Albert C. *Theology in the Wesleyan Spirit*. Nashville: Discipleship Resources, 1975.

Podmore, Colin. *The Moravian Church in England, 1728–1760*. Oxford: Clarendon, 1998.

Rack, Henry D. *Reasonable Enthusiast: John Wesley and the Rise of Methodism*. London: Epworth, 1989.

Rankin, Stephen W. "The People Called Methodists." In *From Aldersgate to Azusa Street*, edited by Henry H. Knight III, 36–44. Eugene, OR: Pickwick, 2010.

Rattenbury, J. Ernest. *The Eucharistic Hymns of John and Charles Wesley*. London: Epworth, 1948.

Rogal, Samuel J. *Susanna Annesley Wesley (1669–1742): A Biography of Strength and Love*. Lima, OH: Wyndham Hall, 2001.

Rodes, Stanley J. *From Faith to Faith: John Wesley's Covenant Theology and the Way of Salvation*. Eugene, OR: Pickwick, 2013.

Runyon, Theodore. *The New Creation: John Wesley's Theology Today*. Nashville: Abingdon, 1998.

Rupp, Gordon. *Principalities and Powers: Studies in the Christian Conflict in History*. Nashville: Abingdon-Cokesbury, 1952.

Schlenther, Boyd Stanley. *Queen of the Methodists: The Countess of Huntingdon and the Eighteenth-Century Crisis of Faith and Society*. Durham: Durham Academic Press, 1997.

Stout, Harry S. *The Divine Dramatist: George Whitefield and the Rise of Modern Evangelicalism*. Grand Rapids: Eerdmans, 1991.

Stanglin, Keith D., and Thomas H. McCall. *Jacob Arminius: Theologian of Grace*. Oxford: Oxford University Press, 2012.

Sommer, Elizabeth W. *Serving Two Masters: Moravian Brethren in Germany and North Carolina, 1727–1801*. Lexington: University Press of Kentucky, 2000.

Synan, Vinson. *The Holiness-Pentecostal Tradition: Charismatic Movements in the Twentieth Century*. Grand Rapids: Eerdmans, 1997.

Torpy, Alan Arthur. *The Prevenient Piety of Samuel Wesley, Sr.* Lanham, MD: Scarecrow, 2009.

Trinder, Barrie. "John Fletcher's Parishoners: Reflections on Industrial Revolution and Evangelical Revival in Severn Gorge." In *Religion, Gender, and Industry: Exploring Church and Methodism in a Local Setting*, edited by Geordan Hammond and Peter S. Forsaith, 25–37. Eugene, OR: Pickwick, 2011.

Bibliography

Tyson, John R. *Assist Me to Proclaim: The Life and Hymns of Charles Wesley*. Grand Rapids: Eerdmans, 2007
———, ed. *Charles Wesley: A Reader*. New York: Oxford, 1989.
———. *Charles Wesley on Sanctification: A Biographical and Theological Study*. Grand Rapids: F. Asbury, 1986.
Watson, Kevin M. *Pursuing Social Holiness: The Band Meeting in Wesley's Thought and Popular Methodist Practice*. Oxford: Oxford University Press, 2014.
Wesley, Charles, 1707-1788. *The Manuscript Journal of the Reverend Charles Wesley, M.A.* 2 vols. Edited by S. T. Kimbrough Jr. and Kenneth G.C. Newport. Nashville: Kingswood, 2008.
Wesley, John. *Explanatory Notes Upon the New Testament*. London: Epworth, 1950.
———. *The Works of John Wesley*. Vol. 1: *Sermons I*. Albert C. Outler, ed. 1984. Bicentennial ed. Nashville: Abingdon, 1984-. [*Works*]
———. *The Works of John Wesley*. Vol. 2: *Sermons II*. Albert C. Outler, ed. 1985. Bicentennial ed. Nashville: Abingdon, 1984-. [*Works*]
———. *The Works of John Wesley*. Vol. 3: *Sermons III*. Albert C. Outler, ed. 1986. Bicentennial ed. Nashville: Abingdon, 1984-. [*Works*]
———. *The Works of John Wesley*. Vol. 4: *Sermons IV*. Albert C. Outler, ed. 1987. Bicentennial ed. Nashville: Abingdon, 1984-. [*Works*]
———. *The Works of John Wesley*. Vol. 9: *The Methodist Societies*. Rupert E. Davies, ed. 1989. Bicentennial ed. Nashville: Abingdon, 1984-. [*Works*]
———. *The Works of John Wesley*. Vol. 10: *The Methodist Societies: The Minutes of Conference*. Henry D. Rack, ed. 2011. Bicentennial ed. Nashville: Abingdon, 1984-. [*Works*]
———. *The Works of John Wesley*. Vol. 11: *The Appeals to Men of Reason and Religion and Certain Related Letters*. Gerald B. Cragg, ed. 1987. Bicentennial ed. Nashville: Abingdon, 1984-. [*Works*]
———. *The Works of John Wesley*. Vol. 12: *Doctrinal and Controversial Treatises I*. Randy L. Maddox, ed. 2012. Bicentennial ed. Nashville: Abingdon, 1984-. [*Works*]
———. *The Works of John Wesley*. Vol. 13: *Doctrinal and Controversial Treatises II*. Paul Wesley Chilcote and Kenneth J. Collins, eds. 2013. Bicentennial ed. Nashville: Abingdon, 1984-. [*Works*]
———. *The Works of John Wesley*. Vol. 18: *Journals and Diaries I (1735-1738)*. W. Reginald Ward and Richard P. Heitzenrater, eds. 1988. Bicentennial ed. Nashville: Abingdon, 1984-. [*Works*]

Bibliography

———. *The Works of John Wesley.* Vol. 19: *Journals and Diaries II (1738-1743).* W. Reginald Ward and Richard P. Heitzenrater, eds. 1990. Bicentennial ed. Nashville: Abingdon, 1984-. [*Works*]

———. *The Works of John Wesley.* Vol. 20: *Journals and Diaries III (1743-1754).* W. Reginald Ward and Richard P. Heitzenrater, eds. 1991. Bicentennial ed. Nashville: Abingdon, 1984-. [*Works*]

———. *The Works of John Wesley.* Vol. 21: *Journals and Diaries IV (1755-1765).* W. Reginald Ward and Richard P. Heitzenrater, eds. 1992. Bicentennial ed. Nashville: Abingdon, 1984-. [*Works*]

———. *The Works of John Wesley.* Vol. 22: *Journals and Diaries V (1765-1775).* W. Reginald Ward and Richard P. Heitzenrater, eds. 1993. Bicentennial ed. Nashville: Abingdon, 1984-. [*Works*]

———. *The Works of John Wesley.* Vol. 25: *Letters I (1721-1739).* Frank Baker, ed. 1980. Bicentennial ed. Nashville: Abingdon, 1984-. [*Works*]

———. *The Works of John Wesley.* Vol. 26: *Letters II (1740-1755).* Frank Baker, ed. 1982. Bicentennial ed. Nashville: Abingdon, 1984-. [*Works*]

———. *The Works of John Wesley.* Vol. 27: *Letters III (1756-1765).* Ted Campbell, ed. 2015. Bicentennial ed. Nashville: Abingdon, 1984-. [*Works*]

———. *The Works of John Wesley, M.A.* Edited by Thomas Jackson. 14 vols. London: Wesleyan Methodist Book Room, 1829-31. Reprint, Grand Rapids: Baker, 1978. [*Works* (J)]

Williams, Colin W. *John Wesley's Theology Today.* Nashville: Abingdon, 1960.

Wynkoop, Mildred Bangs. *A Theology of Love.* Kansas City: Beacon Hill, 1972.

www.ingramcontent.com/pod-product-compliance
Lightning Source LLC
Chambersburg PA
CBHW030858170426
43193CB00009BA/662